Child neglect
in rich nations

Sylvia Ann Hewlett

unicef
United Nations Children's Fund

United Nations Children's Fund
3 UN Plaza, DH-49B
New York, N.Y. 10017
USA

Child neglect in rich nations, Sylvia Ann Hewlett

ISBN: 92-806-3026-1

September 1993

This publication has been printed on recycled paper.

Contents

Preface

Child neglect in rich nations describes how and why some of the wealthiest nations on earth have short-changed children. Poverty and abandonment are now commonplace experiences for children in the rich world. Over the last 15 years two approaches to child welfare have emerged: a neglect-filled 'Anglo-American' model, where market-driven public policies have slashed family benefits and gone a long way towards privatizing child rearing; and a much more supportive 'European' model, where governments have strengthened rather than weakened safety nets for families with children.

The swelling tide of child neglect has potentially disastrous consequences. Business leaders are beginning to be haunted by a widening gap between the supply of, and the demand for, skilled labour. Unless countries such as the United States and the United Kingdom invest in their children on a new and massive scale, a burgeoning human capital deficit will trigger an economic tailspin.

Much of this book focuses on what to do. The techniques and strategies exist. Throughout Western Europe there are policies and programmes that work. Government can step in and transform the financial incentives to reward rather than penalize families with children, and it can alter the rules of the game to make it harder to abandon a child.

This project could not have been completed without the support and encouragement of colleagues. Richard Jolly helped shape the bones of this book, and I thank him for encouraging me to take my ideas into the international arena. At an early stage I presented my work at the International Child Development Centre in Florence, and I am grateful to Andrea Cornia and James Himes for their comments and criticisms. Peter Bell, James Grant, Vicky Haeri, Patricia Hewitt, Jane Hill, Edgar Koh, Samuel Koo, David Miliband, Peggy Shiller, Ruth Spellman and John Williams also offered valuable help, and I thank them all. Some of the US analysis contained in this book appeared in an expanded form in my book *When the Bough Breaks*, which dealt, exclusively, with the American scene.

Sylvia Ann Hewlett
New York, September 1993

A homeless child in wretched temporary housing
looks out on a dim future. In the UK and the US,
estimates are that more than half of all homeless
children fail to attend school regularly.

Poverty amid plenty

Life is becoming harder for children in some key industrialized countries. Slowly but surely over the last 15 years, some of the world's most powerful economies have tilted in an ominous new direction — towards the devaluation of children — flouting the conventional wisdom that child neglect and deprivation have no place in rich nations. Most dramatically in the United States, but also in Australia, Canada, New Zealand and the United Kingdom, a significant number of children are failing to thrive.

The United States has by far the highest percentage of children living in poverty: 20 per cent, which represents a 21 per cent increase since 1970, as shown on page 3. Three other 'Anglo-American' countries — Australia, Canada and the United Kingdom — are at or near the 9 per cent mark. Yet, in most other rich countries, child poverty rates are a fraction of the United States rate.[1] In Western Europe and Japan, for example, child poverty rates typically hover around 2 to 5 per cent.[2]

The problems of children in Anglo-American nations today range from elemental issues of safety and shelter to more complicated issues of psychic health and educational performance. Child poverty rates, school drop-out rates and teenage suicide rates are all on the rise. In the United States, Scholastic Aptitude Test (SAT) scores for college-bound students are 70 points lower than they were 20 years ago. In the United Kingdom, the number of adolescents taking their own lives grew by 41 per cent during the 1980s. In New Zealand, the number of reported child-abuse cases has doubled in six years. And in Australia, the number of homeless children has increased by a third since 1980. According to one recent blue-ribbon committee, "Never before has one generation of children been less healthy, less cared for or less prepared for life than their parents were at the same age."[3]

These tendencies are particularly ironic given the new level of public commitment to children by world leaders. At the World Summit for Children, held in September 1990 at United Nations Headquarters in New York and attended by approximately half the world's Presidents and Prime Ministers, governments formally adopted a set of goals to improve the life circumstances of children. These included controlling major childhood diseases, halving the incidence of child malnutrition and reducing by a third the death rate in children under five years old. Most countries agreed to draw up national programmes of action to implement the goals.

Despite such impressive initiatives, a large gap between rhetoric and reality remains. A case in point: The 1990 World Summit urged all countries to ratify the Convention on the Rights of the Child, a document seeking to lay down minimum standards for the survival, protection and development of all children. As of 31 August 1993, 146 nations had ratified it; the United States has yet to do so. But without the full commitment to young people of the world's richest democracy, we cannot go beyond "the

"Never before has one generation of children been less healthy, less cared for or less prepared for life than their parents were at the same age."

edge of a new era of concern for the silent and invisible tragedy that poverty inflicts on today's children and on tomorrow's world."[4]

The root causes of child neglect in rich nations have to do with new forms of scarcity in both public resources and parental time. In the financial sphere, policy makers display a weak and eroding commitment to children. For example, during the 1980s, governments pursuing laissez-faire policies reduced housing budgets, cut back on welfare payments to poor families and denied large numbers of working mothers the right to spend a few weeks at home with their newborn babies.

In the United States during that decade, less than 5 per cent of the federal budget was spent on programmes that supported families with children, while approximately 24 per cent of federal resources was spent on persons over the age of 65.[5] Canada followed a similar pattern. By 1990, per capita government spending on senior citizens was 2.7 times greater than that allocated to the young.[6] In these two countries, at least, the resources invested at the beginning of life are now dwarfed by the resources consumed at the end of life. American and Canadian policy makers have tended to socialize the costs of growing old and to privatize childhood at a time when fragile family structures make it particularly difficult for parents to carry the entire child-raising load.

In the Anglo-American world, this failure to invest public money in children has been aggravated by a growing time deficit. Over the last two decades there has been a sharp decline in the amount of time parents spend caring for their children, a trend that has been particularly pronounced in the United Kingdom and the United States. According to Stanford University economist Victor Fuchs, American children have lost 10 to 12 hours of parental time per week.[7] The time parents have available for their children has been squeezed by the rapid shift of mothers into the paid labour force, by escalating divorce rates and the abandonment of children by their fathers, and by an increase in the number of hours required on the job. In the United States, the average worker is now at work 163 hours a year more than in 1967, which adds up to an extra month of work annually.[8] In a similar vein, time spent on the job in the United Kingdom increased by two hours a week during the 1980s.[9]

Much of this new parental time pressure is, of course, involuntary, provoked by falling wage rates and escalating housing costs. But whatever the reasons behind the parental time deficit, it has had extremely negative effects on children. Unsupervised 'latchkey' children are at increased risk of substance abuse, and children with little or no contact with their fathers are less likely to perform well at school.

The failure to invest either public resources or private time in the raising of children has left millions of youngsters in this important group of Anglo-American cultures fending for themselves, and coping more or less badly with the difficult business of growing up in the 1990s. True, many children continue to be raised in supportive communities by thoughtful, attentive parents; but looming larger is the overall drift, in both government policy and private adult choices, towards blighting youngsters and stunting their potential. An anti-child spirit is loose in these lands.

The root causes of child neglect in rich nations have to do with new forms of scarcity in both public resources and parental time.

In contrast, the negative trends have not extended to continental Europe — or to Japan, for that matter. In the traditionally Catholic countries of southern Europe, families and communities have remained strong enough to continue to provide a supportive environment for raising children, despite some slippage over the last decade. And in the welfare states of Scandinavia, comprehensive and aggressive social policies have compensated for family disintegration and created conditions that allow children to flourish. What these nations share is a wider and deeper vision of collective responsibility for children.

Child poverty in rich nations: Where taxes and transfers help the least

The UK and the US have the highest child poverty rates among the eight industrialized countries shown below — 27.9% and 22.3% respectively of their children 17 years or younger live below 40% of the adjusted median family income, according to 1986 figures. France also has a high child poverty rate — 21.2%, according to 1984 data. However, while France and the other continental European countries reduce their child poverty rates significantly through taxes and transfers, in the US the rate goes down only 1.9% to 20.4% after families receive all forms of cash income plus food stamps and other benefits and pay their taxes (if any). Direct comparison of income and poverty across a wide range of countries was made possible by the Luxembourg Income Study (LIS) database.

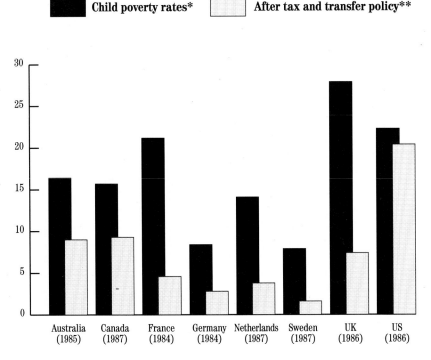

■ **Child poverty rates***   ▦ **After tax and transfer policy****

Poverty rates measured as percentages of children living below 40% of the adjusted median family income in each country.

*The ratio of the US poverty line for a three-person family to the adjusted median income was 40.7% in 1986. Thus, the 40% line is close to the official US poverty line.

**Includes all forms of cash income plus food stamps and similar benefits in other nations, minus federal income and payroll taxes.

Income is adjusted using the US poverty line equivalence scale.

Source: Timothy M. Smeeding, 'The War on Poverty: What Worked?' Testimony to the Joint Economic Committee, the United States Congress, 25 September 1991.

A two-year-old child in a rural homeless shelter
endures not only the loss of security and continuity
a home provides, but also the possible dissolution
of her family.

Disturbing trends

The lives of children in industrialized countries improved significantly in the period immediately following the Second World War. Indeed, the quarter-century between 1950 and 1975 has been called the golden age of social development. During those years, sustained economic growth combined with an expanding welfare state and stable families to dramatically improve the life chances of children. Western Europe achieved the fastest reduction in infant mortality ever recorded, lowering the rate per 1,000 live births from 44 in 1950 to 9 in 1990. At the same time, secondary school enrolment rates increased significantly, rising from 35 to 76 per cent of that age group in Italy and from 39 to 98 per cent in the then Federal Republic of Germany.[10]

In the mid-1970s, structural conditions began to change and governments — particularly in the Anglo-American world — became less attentive to the needs of children. Progress in child welfare slackened and in some key areas trends were dramatically reversed. The old scourge of child poverty re-emerged, and this time material deprivation was compounded by more complicated problems, including underperformance at school, substance abuse, out-of-wedlock births, teenage suicides and severe eating disorders. Now, even privileged youngsters seem increasingly overwhelmed "by drugs, pregnancy, bad grades and bad jobs."[11]

The factors behind these disturbing developments are complex. Economic growth slowed significantly in the mid-1970s. In market economies, growth in gross domestic product (GDP) per capita fell sharply from an average of 4-5 per cent in the 1950s and 1960s to 1-2 per cent in the 1980s. The slow-down in growth was associated with increases in inflation and unemployment, and with growing inequality and low pay — all of which had a detrimental effect on the circumstances of families with children. Falling wage rates were especially harmful.

Shrinking wages

The period from 1975 to 1990 saw a startling increase in the number of low-wage jobs, particularly in Anglo-American economies, where poor educational standards and inadequate 'human capital' encouraged deindustrialization and the proliferation of low-productivity service-sector jobs.

In the United States, for example, the male wage fell 19 per cent between 1973 and 1987. Wives and mothers flooded into the labour market in an attempt to shore up family income, but most American families ultimately found themselves working much harder for approximately the same income. In 1988, average family income was only 6 per cent higher than in 1973, even though a third more married women were now in the labour force.[12] In many households, one well-paid factory job has been replaced by two marginal service-sector jobs. Burger King simply does not pay as well as the Ford Motor Company. Congresswoman Pat Schroeder, in describing the need for modern families to work twice as hard to stay even, has noted that "like the hamster in the wheel, they run and run and run, but they're still at the bottom."[13]

The wage crisis has not been confined to the United States. In Australia, for example, average real earnings declined by 29 Australian dollars a week between 1984 and 1989 — despite the fact that the Australian gross national product (GNP) grew at a rate of 4.5 per cent a year during that period. As might be expected, declining wages triggered a rapid rise in the number of working wives and mothers. Between 1980 and 1989, the number of married women in the paid labour force grew by 40 per cent in Australia. Among couples with dependent children, the proportion with both partners employed rose from 42 per cent at the beginning of the decade to 57 per cent at the end.

In contrast with the shrinking wage levels typical of the Anglo-American world, many European countries experienced a steady increase in wage rates in the last decade. For instance, in the then Federal Republic of Germany, real hourly earnings in manufacturing increased by 1.3 per cent a year during the 1980s, while in France, wages increased by 0.9 per cent a year.[14]

Time and the two-income family

Largely because of these economic pressures, which have been particularly acute in the Anglo-American world, parents are devoting much more time to earning a living and much less time to their children than they did a generation ago. Victor Fuchs has shown that, in the United States, parental time available to children fell appreciably between 1960 and 1986: "On average, in white households with children, there were 10 hours less per week of potential parental time ... while the decrease for black households with children was even greater, approximately 12 hours per week."[15] A prime cause of this fall-off in parental time has been the enormous shift of women into the labour force. In 1960, 30 per cent of American women worked; by 1988, 66 per cent were in the paid labour force. In Europe, trends have been similar. By the late 1980s, 62 per cent of British women, 80 per cent of Swedish women and 59 per cent of French women were in the paid workforce.

University of Maryland sociologist John Robinson has shown that the more hours mothers are employed, the fewer hours they can give to 'primary care activities' such as playing with and talking to children; dressing, feeding and chauffeuring them; and helping them with homework. According to Robinson, employed mothers spend an average of six hours each week in primary child-care activities — just under half the time logged by non-employed mothers and twice that of fathers (employed or non-employed). Robinson points out that wage labour not only eats into primary care but also influences the total amount of contact parents have

In the Anglo-American world, parents are devoting much more time to earning a living and much less time to their children than they did a generation ago.

with their children. The data show that the amount of 'total contact time' (defined as 'all time parents spend with children, including time spent doing other things') has dropped 40 per cent during the last quarter-century.[16] The drop is significant because many of the things parents do with children, whether it is visiting grandma or shopping for groceries, play an important role in building strong parent-child relationships and in giving families a shared identity.

It is important to stress that growing economic pressure on families with children, particularly young families and single parents, is at the heart of the parental time shortage. Many families are squeezed on two fronts, dealing with falling wages, while at the same time they are also facing sharply higher living costs. In the United States, mortgage payments now eat up 29 per cent of median family income, up from 17 per cent in 1970, while college tuition consumes 40 per cent of family income, up from 29 per cent in 1970.[17]

Trends are similar in the United Kingdom. House prices there tripled between 1970 and 1990; indeed, for first-time house buyers, mortgage payments now consume 40 per cent of net household income, up from 18 per cent in 1970.[18] It is no wonder that most British families need both parents in the labour force.

Longer work weeks

If children are affected adversely when both parents work outside the home, their problems are exacerbated by the structural changes that have increased the number of hours both mothers and fathers spend on the job. Americans are working harder than ever. According to a recent survey, the average work week jumped from 41 hours in 1973 to 47 hours in 1989.[19] In better-paying, more prestigious jobs, time demands have become truly impressive. Entrepreneurs in small businesses are now working 57.3 hours a week; professionals, 52.2 hours a week; and those with incomes over US$50,000 a year, 52.4 hours a week. A 1988 survey by *The Wall Street Journal* found that 88 per cent of senior executives worked 10 or more hours a day, and 18 per cent worked 12 or more hours. On average, these top executives were working three hours a week more than they did 10 years ago and were taking two days less vacation each year.[20]

These long hours are not the result of some collective pathology. Rather, there are new and highly rational reasons why people are working so hard. Harvard University economist Rosabeth Kanter linked the longer work week with the manner in which the workplace changed in the deregulated, newly competitive environment of the 1980s.[21]

The most obvious pressure emanates from a new level of employment insecurity. During much of the 1980s, the United States labour market was in turmoil. In an effort to become more competitive, hundreds of corporations rushed to restructure — merging operations, purging employees, buying this company, selling off that division. In the space of four years, from 1983 to 1987, more than 2 million people saw their jobs disappear or deteriorate as a result of mergers and acquisitions. No industry was immune. The semiconductor industry, for example, a star performer in the early 1980s, laid off nearly 25,000 employees after losses of US$2 billion in the mid-1980s. Overall, more than 13 million Americans lost their jobs between 1981 and 1990. Two thirds of the people laid off eventually found new jobs, but almost half of the new jobs paid less than the old ones.

Clearly, the threat of unemployment, and the knowledge that any new job is likely to involve a wage cut, has led many employees to work longer hours to show how indispensable they are. In the words of one middle-level manager, "When you see people being laid off all around you, you'd have to be irrational not to put your nose to the grindstone."[22]

The cult of the workaholic has spread to the United Kingdom. London's Low Pay Unit reports that the British male now works five hours more per week than his continental counterpart. A recent survey of 200 British executives found that they worked an average of 55 hours a week. Fewer than half took their full holiday entitlement, and 25 per cent worked every weekend. Advertising campaigns for upscale British cars exploit the 'chic' overtones of working long hours. In the words of one commercial: "It's tough at the top. When you're indispensable, working late is the rule rather than the exception. But look on the bright side, you'll have the road to yourself on the way home."[23]

Long hours seem to have little appeal elsewhere in Europe, a fact highlighted in a 1992 study of the formation of British Petroleum's multinational office in Brussels. Working hours became a highly controversial issue among the 40 senior staff. American and British managers equated long hours with commitment to the corporation. Scandinavian managers saw long hours as a sign of incompetence, suggesting that employees caught at their desks after 4.30 p.m. needed help or training. And German managers insisted that employees be judged by the quality of their output rather than by the simple input of time.

Relaxed European attitudes towards the work week have been greatly facilitated by a powerful trade union movement that has kept the issue of shorter hours at the top of the agenda throughout the postwar period. In bad economic times, unions have resisted the inevitable pressure for longer hours, arguing that a shorter work week actually combats unemployment by spreading the work around. Even during the severe downturn of the early and mid-1980s, weekly hours for most European workers continued to fall. Only recently, the large German union IG Metall won a 35-hour work week for its members, a gain that is expected to spread through the German labour force. And vacation time continues to rise throughout Europe. Recent collective-bargaining agreements have set annual paid leave at five to six weeks in France and six weeks in Germany. Contrast this to the American scene, where in 1989, workers had an average of 16 days off, down from 20 days in 1981.

Moreover, the worlds of work and of the family have become particularly incompatible in the United States, where children spend 25 per cent fewer hours in school than their European counterparts, while at the same time their parents work longer hours and enjoy shorter vaca-

In the United States, children spend 25 per cent fewer hours in school than their European counterparts.

tions than European parents. In the United States, the typical school day lasts six hours and the school year 180 days, while in Europe the average school day lasts eight hours and the school year 220 days. The lack of synchronization between school hours and work hours is hard on youngsters. By and large, the vacuum left in children's lives by the retreat of the traditional home-maker has not been filled with attentive fathers, quality child care, expanded educational programmes or any other worthwhile activity. In large measure, the void has been filled by television. The average American teenager now spends four times as many hours watching television as doing homework.

Stress and strain

So far, the parental time deficit has been discussed as a decline in the amount of time parents spend with their children. But the parent-child relationship depends on qualitative as well as quantitative factors, and in the early 1990s severe time constraints are compounded by mounting job-related stress. In contemporary Anglo-American societies, children not only have two parents at work, they also have mothers as well as fathers who routinely work 55-hour weeks and who come home preoccupied and exhausted, unable to give much of anything to their children. If one has been biting the bullet all day at the office — meeting deadlines, rushing orders, humouring the boss — it can be difficult to devote quality time to children in the evening.

Research by Pittman and Brooks has shown that the hard-edged personality traits cultivated by many successful professionals — control, decisiveness, aggressiveness, efficiency — can be directly at odds with the passive, patient, selfless elements in good nurturing.[24] The last thing a 3-year-old or a 13-year-old needs at 8 o'clock in the evening is a mother — or father, for that matter — who marches into the house in his or her power suit, barking orders, and looking and sounding like a drill sergeant.

Compare the ingredients in a recipe for career success with those of a recipe for meeting the needs of a child, beginning with the all-important ingredient of time. To succeed in one's career may require long hours and consume one's best energy, leaving little time to spend together as a family and precious little enthusiasm for the hard tasks of parenting. Mobility and a prime commitment

With economic pressures, job-related stress and time demands, US parents increasingly fall back on television to keep their children entertained.

Unsupervised 'latchkey' children are at increased risk of substance abuse.

to oneself are virtues in the job world; stability, selflessness and a commitment to others are virtues in family life. Qualities needed for career success also include efficiency, a controlling attitude, an orientation towards the future and an inclination towards perfection, while their virtual opposites — tolerance for mess and disorder, an ability to let go, an appreciation of the moment, and an acceptance of difference and failure — are what is needed for successful parenting.

Not all high achievers display the goal-oriented, time-pressured approach associated with career success, and not all good parents are endowed with unlimited stores of patience and humour. But most professionals and most parents will recognize some of these qualities in themselves. Most are also aware that the aptitudes, skills and talents that people hone to become successful professionals may not stand them in good stead when they assume the role of parent. And the struggle to span the divide between family and work can be painful and fraught with failure for both parent and child. It is one thing to pound along home at seven o'clock in the evening and somehow find the time to help a child with a homework assignment; it is quite something else to summon the energy and the attitudes that enable one to be a constructive presence. Many high-powered parents find it extremely hard to switch gears.

It is a telling comment on the state of affairs that Hallmark, the greeting card company, now markets cards for overcommitted professional parents who find it difficult to actually see their children. "Have a super day at school," chirps one card meant to be left under the cereal box in the morning. "I wish I were there to tuck you in," says another, designed to peek out from behind the pillow at night.

Fallout on children

Recent research has uncovered ominous links between absentee parents and a range of behavioural problems in children. A 1989 study that surveyed 5,000 eighth-grade students (14-year-olds) in the San Diego and Los Angeles areas found that the more hours children took care of themselves each week, the greater the risk of substance abuse.[25] In fact, latchkey children as a group were twice as likely to drink alcohol or take drugs as were children under the supervision of an adult after school. The increased risk of substance abuse held true regardless of the child's sex, race, family income, academic performance or number of resident parents. All that mattered was how many hours the child was left on his or her own.

Another surprising finding of the southern California study is that it was the white children from affluent homes who spent the largest number of hours on their own. Children from upper-income professional families seem more likely to have mothers as well as fathers who invest long hours in their careers and come home at 7 or 8 o'clock, tired and distracted.

Absentee fathers

While the welfare of children is being compromised by a new and more rigorous set of work pressures, it is also being jeopardized by burgeoning divorce rates, sharp increases in out-of-wedlock births and a striking rise in the number of fatherless households. All of these disturbing trends are most pronounced in the Anglo-American world.

For children, experiencing divorce and single parenthood, as well as the absence of their fathers, remain major traumas.

The divorce rate in the United States is by far the highest in the world: In 1990, 5.3 divorces were granted for every 1,000 people. In the United Kingdom, the figure was 3.2; in Canada 2.6; in Sweden 2.4; in France 1.6; and in Italy 0.2. Fifteen million American children, one quarter of all children under 18, are now growing up without fathers — 10 million as a result of marital breakdown and 5 million as a result of out-of-wedlock births. The absence of fathers is twice as common as it was a generation ago, and no relief is on the horizon. In l960, 11 per cent of American children lived with their mother alone; by l989, the figure had reached 26 per cent.[26]

In the United Kingdom, the trend developed even more rapidly. During the 1980s, the number of out-of-wedlock births doubled, and by 1990, 25 per cent of all babies were born to single mothers. The disintegration of the traditional family has proceeded at a much more rapid pace in the United Kingdom than in the rest of Europe.

Despite our new familiarity with family breakdown, for children, experiencing divorce and single parenthood, as well as the absence of their fathers, remain major traumas. Over the past decade, research by Weitzman, Wallerstein, Duncan, Furstenberg and others has shown the effects of divorce on children to be unexpectedly profound and long-lasting.

For one thing, evidence from a number of countries, especially the United Kingdom and the United States, shows the financial repercussions of divorce on children to be extremely serious. The economic harm to children from the divorce of their parents arises from the fact that fathers generally earn a good deal more than mothers, but in approximately 90 per cent of cases, children remain with their mothers after divorce. Non-custodial fathers are, of course, expected to contribute their share to the costs of raising a child by paying child support to the mother, but a substantial number of divorcing men (approximately 40 per cent in the

United Kingdom and the United States) walk away from marriage without a child support agreement. Even when an agreement is in place, child support payments tend to be low and unreliable. Despite increasingly tough enforcement laws, a recent American survey found that only 51 per cent of mothers entitled to child support received the full amount, 25 per cent received partial payment and 23 per cent received nothing at all. In the United States, US$4.6 billion is now owed by fathers to the children of divorce.[27]

Along with the problem of collection, there is also the problem of the low level of child support awards. In the United States, the average yearly amount of child support paid to a divorced woman and her children is only US$2,710 a year. Even if the sum is paid regularly, it covers less than a quarter of the average annual cost of raising one child. Inadequate child support combines with low female earnings to produce a situation in which the income of ex-wives and their dependent children plummets after divorce. According to Duncan and Hoffmann, on average, a woman's standard of living drops 30 per cent in the five years after divorce.[28]

While the economic fallout of divorce on children has received widespread public attention, the emotional and educational consequences are less well known. There is, however, a great deal of new evidence showing that the breakup of a marriage can trigger severe psychic and behavioural problems in children. Divorce seems capable of derailing a child's progress in school and is often the single most important cause of enduring pain in a child's life. Many of these problems are caused by the fact that the children of divorced parents see very little of their fathers. For all the talk about the new nurturing father, the reality for many youngsters is quite the opposite: a father who disappears, abandoning his children financially and emotionally.

The data show minimal contact between non-custodial fathers and their children. Furstenberg and Harris, at the University of Pennsylvania, followed a sample of 1,000 children from disrupted families between 1976 and 1987 and found that 42 per cent had not seen their fathers at all during the previous year. Only 20 per cent had slept at their father's house in the previous month, and only one in six saw their fathers once a week or more.[29] According to Furstenberg, "Men regard marriage as a package deal ... they cannot separate their relations with their children from their relations to their former spouse. When that relationship ends, the paternal bond usually withers."[30]

For most children, the partial or complete loss of a father produces long-lasting feelings of rejection, rage and pain, and can lead to permanent emotional damage. For example, divorce seems to be an important factor in teenage suicide, which has tripled over the last 25 years in both the United Kingdom and the United States and is now the second leading cause of death in the 15- to 24-year-old age group. A study of 752 families by researchers at the New York Psychiatric Institute found that youngsters who attempted suicide differed little from those who did not in terms of age, income, race and religion, but they were much more likely "to live in non-intact family settings" and to have minimal contact with the father.[31] In fact, divorce and the absence of the father play a role in the entire range of adolescent psychological troubles.

In addition to the emotional consequences, there is mounting evidence that family breakdown and absentee fatherhood contribute to educational underperformance and failure. A survey carried out by Columbia University and Bowling Green State University comparing the SAT scores of 295 students from father-absent homes with those of 760 students from father-present homes found that the absence of the father had a "dramatic" negative effect on scores — a result that could not be explained away by differences in income.[32] In a similar vein, a study of 2,500 young men and women by Krein and Beller found that "even after taking into account the lower income of single-parent families, the absence of a father has a significant negative effect on the educational attainment of boys."[33]

All of the new research linking father absence to psychological stress and cognitive deficits in children serves to underline a basic theme: The problems of children in rich nations are far more complicated than the simple failure of governments to invest enough money in disadvantaged children. Granted, the resource deficit is severe and expanding, but millions of middle-class children are failing to thrive because their parents are either unable or unwilling to provide enough time and attention. There are obvious qualitative differences between a harried single mother who fails to spend time with her children because she is working at two jobs to pay the rent, and a divorced father who shuts his children out of his life to spend time with a new partner. But whether a child is rejected out of hand or merely left alone for large chunks of the day, the results are almost never good. Children do not do well when deprived of parental time and attention.

There is no one recipe for raising children. Harvard University psychologist Jerome Kagan tells us that precisely how a parent feeds an infant, hugs a toddler or interacts with a teenager is less important than "the melody those actions comprise."[34] Even more critical is ensuring adequate time. If a divorced father has not seen his son in six months, it is hard for him to be a constructive presence in the child's life. Melodies cannot work their magic unless they are given time and space.

There is mounting evidence that family breakdown and absentee fatherhood contribute to educational underperformance and failure.

Many busy parents park their children in front of the television for hours each day. Growing economic pressure on families with children is at the heart of the parental time shortage.

Policies and problems

In Anglo-American societies, the stress and strain on family life triggered by shrinking wages, the employment of both parents and marital breakdown have not been counterbalanced by new and more generous benefits and services. On the contrary, support for families has lost ground to other priorities recently. In the 1980s, the proportion of public money spent on families and children was reduced, and even more responsibility was returned to the family — despite the manifest erosion in the family's ability to shoulder these responsibilities. There is probably no way policy makers can protect children from the earthquake that has shuddered through the family over the last 20 years, but rather than responding with generous support, governments in the Anglo-American world, in tightening the purse-strings, have increased the penalties attached to child-raising, albeit unintentionally.

In the United States, 60 per cent of American working women still have no benefits or job protection when they give birth to a child. In the United Kingdom, only 2 per cent of child care available for children under age three is publicly funded. In Canada, 5 billion Canadian dollars (one Canadian dollar = US$0.76, 1 September 1993) have been removed from social programmes that benefited poor children. In all three countries, the claims of families with children have been subordinated to other needs.

A dramatic feature of United States public policy is the way in which the Government has intervened on behalf of the elderly but not on behalf of children. According to figures compiled by Timothy Smeeding (see overleaf), from 1984 to 1987 the same tax policy and income transfers in the United States (including health and housing subsidies) that reduced the rate of poverty among the elderly from 46 per cent to 11 per cent, have reduced child poverty by only 2 per cent, taking the rate from 22 to 20 per cent.[35] Indeed, the United States Government now allocates an average sum of US$9,500 in federal subsidies to each elderly person, but only US$870 to each child. It is small wonder that the poverty rate among American children is now twice as high as among the elderly.[36]

Canadian public policy has followed a similar path. Government transfer payments now account for 52 per cent of the income of seniors, up from 44 per cent in the 1970s. As a result, the proportion of seniors in poverty is now one half of what it was in 1980. There has been no corresponding reduction in child poverty rates, however. On the contrary, in 1990, child poverty was two percentage points higher than in 1980. A large part of the problem is the low level of public support for families with children. Real income from government programmes for children has been declining; income support per child averaged 751 Canadian dollars in 1989, down from 913 in 1978.[37]

The situation in Europe is quite different from that in the United States and Canada. In France, for example, in recent years, tax policy and income transfers have reduced poverty among the elderly by a decisive 75

Poverty rates of children in eight industrialized countries

Tax and transfer policy in the eight industrialized countries shown below leaves children (17 years or under) no better off than adults and worse off than those aged 65 or above — often by a big margin. These mid-1980s data show that income security measures reduce child poverty by an average of 9.4% but cut senior citizen poverty by 60.7% (or over six times more). The US has the worst disparity in this regard. It reduces child poverty by 1.9% but decreases poverty among the elderly by 35.6% (or nearly 19 times more). Even children in single-parent families in these eight countries are left worse off than senior citizens by such measures: Their poverty is reduced by an average of 33.7% compared to 60.7% for those aged 65 or above. Direct comparison of income and poverty across a wide range of countries was made possible by the Luxembourg Income Study (LIS) database.

	Australia 1985	Canada 1987	France 1984	Germany 1984	Netherlands 1987	Sweden 1987	UK 1986	US 1986	Average
All People									
Pre *	19.1	17.1	26.4	21.6	21.5	25.9	27.7	19.9	22.4
Post **	6.7	7.0	4.5	2.8	3.4	4.3	5.2	13.3	5.9
Change	-12.4	-10.1	-21.9	-18.8	-18.1	-21.6	-22.5	-6.6	-16.5
Aged 65 or older									
Pre	54.5	50.2	76.2	80.1	56.1	83.2	62.1	46.5	63.6
Post	4.0	2.2	0.7	3.8	0.0	0.7	1.0	10.9	2.9
Change	-50.5	-48.0	-75.5	-76.3	-56.1	-82.5	-61.1	-35.6	-60.7
Adults (18-64)									
Pre	12.9	11.5	17.6	9.8	17.4	13.4	18.1	12.8	14.2
Post	6.1	7.0	5.2	2.6	3.9	6.6	5.3	10.5	5.9
Change	-6.8	-4.5	-12.4	-7.2	-13.5	-6.8	-12.8	-2.3	-8.3
Children (17 or younger)									
Pre	16.4	15.7	21.1	8.4	14.1	7.9	27.9	22.3	16.7
Post	9.0	9.3	4.6	2.8	3.8	-1.6	7.4	20.4	7.4
Change	-7.4	-6.4	-16.5	-5.6	-10.3	-6.3	-20.5	-1.9	-9.4
Children with one parent									
Pre	70.2	56.6	43.1	46.0	70.3	23.2	71.2	58.1	54.8
Post	34.6	37.1	13.1	15.9	3.8	2.0	8.5	54.2	21.2
Change	-35.6	-19.5	-30.0	-30.1	-66.5	-21.2	-62.7	-3.9	-33.7
Other children									
Pre	11.3	11.7	19.4	6.9	9.2	5.2	22.2	15.7	12.7
Post	6.6	6.6	4.0	2.3	3.8	1.5	7.3	14.1	5.7
Change	-4.7	-5.1	-15.4	-4.6	-5.4	-3.7	-14.9	-1.6	6.9

Poverty rates measured as percentages of children living below 40% of the adjusted median family income in each country.

* Pre tax and transfer income compares family income based on earnings, property income and private transfers (e.g., private pensions, alimony and child support) to 40% of the adjusted median family income in each country.

** Post tax and transfer income includes the effect of direct taxes, including negative taxes such as the US Earned Income Tax Credit, and public transfers on poverty.

Source: Timothy M. Smeeding, 'The War on Poverty: What Worked?' Testimony to the Joint Economic Committee, the United States Congress, 25 September 1991.

per cent, taking the rate from 76 to 0.7 per cent; but poverty among children has also been reduced significantly, falling from 21 to 5 per cent. Similarly, in the Netherlands, public policies have reduced poverty among the elderly by an impressive 56 per cent, taking the rate from 56 per cent to zero, while these same policies have lowered the child poverty rate from 14 to 4 per cent.[38]

Shortfalls in funding

Housing and health care are two policy areas where the allocation of generous amounts of public money is capable of making a great deal of difference to the well-being of families with children. Unlike most European countries, the United Kingdom and the United States do not fund these services at levels that guarantee universal access.

In the United States, federal support for low-income housing dropped from US$32 billion in 1978 to US$9 billion in 1988, a decline of more than 80 per cent after adjusting for inflation.[39] The cut-back is the main cause of an acute housing shortage that now stretches across the nation. Estimates vary, but in the early 1990s, somewhere between 600,000 and 3 million people are homeless. Approximately 30 per cent of them are families, most often a parent with two or three children. The average child is 6 years old; the average parent, 27. The loss of a home often leads to the dissolution of a family: two older children in foster care, the wife and baby in a public shelter, the husband sleeping on a park bench or under a bridge.

Homelessness can be a devastating experience for a child, because a home is much more than four walls and a roof. A home provides warmth, security and continuity. Homeless children quickly lose their emotional anchor — and their chance at an education. In the United Kingdom and the United States, local authorities estimate that more than half of all homeless children fail to attend school on a regular basis.

The growing ranks of the homeless are merely the most visible indicator of the contemporary housing shortage. In 1989, 10 million Americans were living near the edge of homelessness, doubled up with friends or family. The arrival of a new baby, a landlord's displeasure or simply rising tensions due to overcrowding could cost these people a place to live. According to Barry Zigas, Director of the National Low Income Coalition in Washington, D.C., conditions are "the worst since the Great Depression."[40] Local officials report that there is no public housing available for hundreds of thousands of poor families who, under existing government regulations, qualify for help. There are today about 44,000 persons on the waiting list in Chicago, 60,000 in Miami and 200,000 in New York City.

While approximately 330,000 children are homeless in the United States, 12 million are uninsured and have little or no access to health care. During the 1980s, growing numbers of families with children fell through the medical safety net. The reasons are simple: Since 1980, far fewer families have been able to rely on company-sponsored insurance to take

Housing and health care are two policy areas where the allocation of generous amounts of public money is capable of making a great deal of difference to the well-being of families with children.

A homeless family living in a shelter in California reflects the increasing rates of child poverty in the US, where 1990 per capita government spending on senior citizens was 27 times greater than that allocated to the young.

care of their health needs, and government programmes, especially Medicaid, have been cut back.

During the 1980s, the number of uninsured Americans rose by one fifth, from 30 million in 1980 to 37 million in 1987.[41] More parents are working at low-wage service-sector jobs that offer no benefits. Medicaid is intended to help uninsured low-income families to cover their health costs, but today such families are unlikely to get help unless their income is at or below the eligibility level of Aid for Families with Dependent Children (AFDC) — often considerably below the poverty line — and their children are under six years old. In 1990, the Medicaid system financed health care for only 40 per cent of those below the poverty line, compared with 65 per cent in the mid-1970s. Families with children who do not qualify for Medicaid must rely on a patchwork of public health programmes that fail to serve the eligible population because of a shortfall in public funds. For example, the nation's 550 community health centres serve only 5 million patients each year, leaving 20 million eligible people, two thirds of them mothers and children, without such services. Funding for Title V (the maternal and child health programme targeted at the uninsured) is now so low that fewer than half of all states are able to offer prenatal programmes on a statewide basis, and only a handful of states can pay for hospital delivery services for low-income uninsured women.

Current American policies do not emphasize the importance of prenatal and maternity care. The resulting statistics speak for themselves. In 1991, 40,000 babies died before their first birthday, and half of the deaths could have been avoided because they were the direct result of mothers receiving little or no prenatal care. It has been shown that women who do not receive adequate prenatal care are 40 times more likely to lose their baby in the first month of life than those who initiate prenatal care in the critical first three months of pregnancy.[42] They are also three times as likely to have premature, low-birth-weight babies. Infants who weigh less than 5.5 pounds at birth often need expensive medical attention and are much more likely than full-term babies to suffer lifelong disabilities such as cerebral palsy, seizure disorders, blindness and mental retardation.

None of this pain and suffering comes cheaply. In 1989, the United States Congress estimated the cost of caring for dangerously premature babies at US$2.4 billion annually. Initial hospital costs averaged US$54,000 per child, and the price tag of a lifetime of care and treatment for these children averaged US$389,800.[43]

Yet, despite the enormous savings inherent in effective prenatal care, it is more difficult to obtain today than it was in 1975. Seventeen per cent of American women of child-bearing age do not have medical coverage, up from 12 per cent 10 years ago.

The United States is unique in its lack of provision for childbirth. In all other rich nations, pregnant women and newborn children are treated with much more generosity and humanity — which is a large part of the reason why infant mortality rates are so much lower in France, Japan, the Netherlands and Sweden than they are in the United States.[44]

On the housing front, however, the United States is not alone. In recent years, Australia and the United Kingdom have tended to take the same direction as the United States. In the United Kingdom, housing has suffered the sharpest cuts of all social expenditure, falling from £7 billion in 1978 to £2.7 billion in 1989 (in real terms). This produced a considerable decline in the stock of low-income housing and pushed rents up. The result has been a significant increase in homelessness, particularly among young families. Homelessness doubled during the 1980s, and 79 per cent of homeless households now include children. The number of young runaways aged 16 to 19 who are homeless and living on the streets of large cities has also markedly increased. The problems of these young people can be traced to the shortage of housing, but they are greatly exacerbated by recent changes in the social security rules that have removed entitlements from 16- and 17-year-olds. Many youngsters who cannot rely on support from their families and who cannot find jobs are now destitute.

A shortage of time

In Australia, the United Kingdom and the United States laissez-faire policies towards families with children have failed miserably in the task of enhancing the amount of time working parents are able to spend with their children. Maternity or parenting leave is a case in point.

In the United States, the only federal provision for pregnancy or maternity is contained in the 1978 Pregnancy Disability Amendment, which decrees that an employer cannot fire a worker solely because she is pregnant and that a pregnant woman is eligible for the same fringe benefits as workers with "other disabilities."[45]

Although this Amendment was hailed as a major victory for women's rights, it affords pregnant women and their newborn children very few protections or benefits. Specifically, it does not guarantee any leave from employment for a mother (or father) to spend time with a newborn child, nor does it direct employers to reinstate women in their jobs after they have recovered from childbirth. The only thing it does provide is six to eight weeks of partial wage replacement at the time of birth if a working woman is covered by temporary disability insurance. However, since only five states require this kind of insurance, experts estimate that 60 per cent

of American working women have no benefits for pregnancy or childbirth.

Recent attempts to improve on the Pregnancy Disability Amendment have run into trouble. In 1990, the House and the Senate finally passed a Family and Medical Leave Bill that would have provided 12 weeks of unpaid, job-protected leave for both male and female employees at the time of birth, but it was vetoed.[46] Despite the fact that 50 per cent of mothers with babies under 12 months old are now in the workforce, the American system has had an extraordinarily difficult time defining childbirth as an appropriate target for legislation, and American Presidents have been loath to regulate employers or interfere with the intimate workings of family life. More recently, one of the first acts of the Clinton Administration was to pass the Family and Medical Leave Act in February 1993, that went into effect on 5 August 1993. However, this has only partially solved the problem since companies with fewer than 50 employees remain exempt, and many American working women are employed by small firms.

The United Kingdom also displays laissez-faire tendencies on the maternity leave front. Along with the rest of the European Community, the United Kingdom mandates a series of rights and benefits around birth, but it then restricts these rights more severely than anywhere else in Europe. In the United Kingdom, women qualify for maternity leave only if they have been in full-time employment with the same employer for two years, or part time for five years. As a result, in 1990, 45 per cent of British working women failed to qualify for benefits.[47] The country has resisted adopting European Community standards in this area, preferring to rely on voluntary private-sector initiatives.

Similarly, Australian provisions for maternity leave are far from comprehensive. A survey conducted by the Australian Institute of Family Studies in the late 1980s found that in the private sector one third of all working women were ineligible for maternity leave or benefits.[48]

In sharp contrast to the restricted maternity benefits typical of the Anglo-American world, a large number of Western European governments provide a generous package of rights and benefits to all working parents when a child is born. For example, Sweden provides a parenting leave of 15 months at the birth of a child, to be taken by either parent, and replaces 90 per cent of earnings up to a specified maximum. In Italy, a pregnant women is entitled to five months of paid leave at 80 per cent of her wage, followed by a further six months at 30 per cent of her wage. Her job is guaranteed for both periods. Perhaps the most remarkable fact about the Italian system is that a woman is entitled to two years of credit towards seniority each time she gives birth to a child. Not only does an Italian woman not get fired for having a child — she is actually rewarded.

An obvious consequence of the absence of comprehensive maternity or parenting leave policies in Anglo-American countries is that children are deprived of parental time and attention during those critical first weeks of life. Most child-rearing experts see six months as the minimally adequate period of time for a parent to bond with a new child.[49] Approximately 30 per cent of American babies and 20 per cent of British babies are deprived of that precious time.

In Anglo-American countries . . . children are deprived of parental time and attention during those critical first weeks of life.

Forging a public morality

Harvard legal scholar Mary Ann Glendon tells us to be wary. We need to be very careful about the "stories we tell," the "symbols we deploy" and the "visions we project" in our public policies, because these ciphers forge the aspirations and identity of the nation, and in so doing, help construct a public morality.[50] This is bad news for those who care about the welfare of children in the Anglo-American world. Take, for example, the story told by American policies at the beginning of life.

Some revealing symbolism is embedded in the language of American labour laws. It is striking that in the United States the only legal provision for childbirth — the most miraculous event in human life — is written in weak, even demeaning, language that defines pregnancy as just another disability in the eyes of the law. Employers are supposed to provide a pregnant woman with the same fringe benefits they provide workers with other disabilities. In 60 per cent of all cases, these benefits amount to nothing.

And there is further poignant symbolism in what policies do not address. Apart from the recently passed Family and Medical Leave Act, American laws, for example, "are silent about any period a mother, or indeed a father, may wish to be at home to care for an infant child,"[51] and this is despite the fact that the majority of new mothers in the United States are now in paid employment. In most other countries, rich and poor, childbirth receives prominent treatment in the law and is the subject of elaborate legislative support.

Finally, American policies promote an almost punitive vision of personal accountability. In the United States, a baby is seen as an item of private consumption, a little like a winter vacation or a second car, and large portions of the costs of child-raising have been privatized. There are a multitude of direct expenses: Prenatal and maternity care, day care and preschools all need to be purchased in the private market-place. And there are significant indirect costs. Because a large number of American women are not entitled to job protection when they give birth to a child, they are often redefined as 'new hires' when they return to work, routinely losing seniority, benefits and pay. This is a large part of the reason why working mothers in the United States lose from 13 to 20 per cent of their earning power after giving birth to a first child.[52]

In extensive interviews in the 1980s, Vance Packard found that, in the United States, "the decision to have a child is met with perhaps less enthusiasm than at any time in our history, except possibly the depression years ... Having a child has changed from being part of the natural flow of life, to an apprehensive act — or even an act of courage."[53]

In other rich democracies, parents are not required to pay such a high price for their children. In continental Europe, for example, the vision of family life and the incentive structure faced by parents are quite different. Charles de Gaulle, the late President of France, once said that motherhood should be regarded as "a social function similar to military service for men, that has to be financially supported by the whole community."[54] This statement dramatizes the French view of children as precious national resources deserving the aid and attention of the community at large. Nations as diverse as Italy, Japan and Sweden have a profound appreciation of the child as the worker and the citizen of the future. Thus, the health, wealth and security of the nation depend on ensuring that each baby gets a good start in life and that societal conditions permit children to flourish. This sense of collective responsibility for children is the source of the elaborate social supports — family allowances, home visits, preschools — that are so common in continental Europe.

Clearly, government possesses the levers for change. It can alter the rules of the game to make it harder to abandon or otherwise neglect a child, and it can transform tax and transfer policy to reward and strengthen, rather than penalize, families with children.

Motherhood should be regarded as "a social function similar to military service for men, that has to be financially supported by the whole community." – Charles de Gaulle, the late President of France.

A vignette:
Through the eyes of children

Fatima, aged six, sank her teeth into my upper arm. "Let go,"
I said sharply, trying to stay calm, "that hurts." She peered up
at me, her black button eyes bright and challenging. She bit
down again, this time much harder. "Fatima," I said slowly
and deliberately, "if you don't let go, I will never let you brush
my hair again." The threat worked; Fatima slowly let go. She
spent a minute looking with pride at the teeth marks and small
drops of blood on my arm and then quickly snatched a brush
from inside my purse, plunked her frail six-year-old body on
my lap, and started to stroke my hair with care and tender-
ness.

We had only known one another for an hour, but I already knew that Fatima loved brushing and braiding my hair. My first thought was that long, straight, Caucasian hair was different and therefore interesting to this small black child. But I soon realized that her fascination with this activity had much more to do with her desperate need for any form of physical intimacy. Biting, braiding, pinching and cuddling all helped fill

the void in a way that games and storytelling didn't. Besides which, with her short attention span, she found it impossible to concentrate on Candyland for longer than three minutes — playing board games was a painful business.

Ernie, the large genial black man who ran the services in the Prince George Hotel ballroom for the Children's Aid Society, filled me in on the family background before I left the hotel that day.

Fatima had four siblings, two older, two younger. Between them, these children had three fathers, none of them currently on the scene. According to Ernie, their mother, Regina, was "totally out of it." She spent most of her waking hours feeding her crack habit. She "weighed at most 95 pounds and jangled all over." The children rarely made it to school as their mother had a hard time getting them down to the hotel lobby early enough to catch the school bus. Instead, they spent their days drifting around the hallways of the hotel. The oldest, Tyrone, a boy of 10, already spent much of his time on the streets.

The Prince George Hotel where Fatima lived, was, in 1988, a welfare hotel occupied by some 800 homeless families. Located on Madison Avenue at 28th Street in New York City, amid quiet residential streets, publishing houses and coffee-shops, it was a maelstrom of noise and action in a genteel part of town. Mothers stood around, joking and bickering with one another, and children were everywhere. Circling the edges were a few men, some of them sharply dressed. They seemed to be sizing up the women, hoping to strike a deal for either drugs or sex.

Every Tuesday in the summer of 1988 I edged through this crowd, on the way to my duties in the ballroom. I was one of several volunteers from my church. Each of us spent three to six hours a week helping these homeless hotel children with their schoolwork, playing 'educational' games, or just giving individual kids some special attention.

I always dreaded entering the hotel. The guards were invariably hostile, pushing you about with rough hands as they searched you, keeping you waiting for as long as 20 minutes as they checked identification. In addition, the entrance of the Prince George Hotel was a menacing place. Violence was pervasive. Small ugly incidents were constantly erupting on the steps or in the lobby and hallways.

I remember one such ugly incident. It was a beautiful summer's day in early June. Because of the warm weather the hotel steps were particularly crowded, and I stood in line waiting my turn to go through the revolving door. "Shut your f–––mouth," one mother bellowed a few feet to my right. I jumped nervously, wondering if she was yelling at me. But she grabbed a three-year-old boy and started slapping his face, quite viciously, I thought. The boy thought otherwise. "It don't hurt, Mom," he crowed between each slap, goading her on. "You goddam brat," screamed his mother and set to work with a series of more powerful blows. I winced as blood started to leak from the boy's mouth and, taking advantage of a gap in the crowd (people had moved to the side to get a better view of the stand-off between mother and son), quickly scuttled into the hotel to fetch a guard — who, after surveying the scene, shrugged his shoulders and walked away.

A kid with a bloody face was small potatoes by Prince George standards. Just that month there had been two homicides and five drug-related knifings that I knew of. All of these welfare hotels in midtown were immensely violent. In one particularly tragic case at the Martinique Hotel, a 10-month-old baby girl was found dead in a hotel room. When she died Tamara weighed less than seven pounds. The proximate causes of death were premature birth, poor nutrition and an intestinal infection. The underlying reasons for her needless death ranged from poverty and homelessness to parental neglect. A few weeks after the baby's death, her big brother, eight-year-old Brian, dictated a poem to a volunteer worker at the hotel:

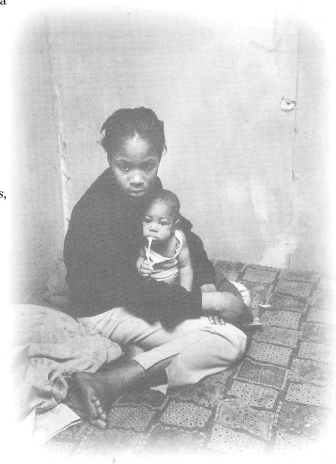

> When our baby die we start to
> sit by the window. We just
> sit an' sit, all wrapped up
> quiet in old shirts an' watch
> the pigeons. That pigeon she fly so
> fast, move so fast. She move nice.
> A real pretty flyer.
>
> She open her mouth and take in
> the wind. We just spread out crumbs,
> me and my brother. And we wait.
> Sit and wait.
> There under the windowsill.
>
> She don't even see us till we slam
> down the window. And she break.
> She look with one eye.
> She don't die right away.
> We dip her in, over and over,
> in the water pot we boils on
> the hot plate.
>
> We wanna see how it be to die
> slow like our baby die.

I showed this poem to one of the social workers at the Prince George. Her reaction was bitter: "We are breeding expensive killers in these homeless hotels, and no one seems to care." An understandable response given the current costs of child neglect in New York City.

A recent study estimated that in the United States the costs to the taxpayer of one 'throwaway child' — a child like Brian who, at age eight, has already dropped out of school — is about US$300,000. That is the cost of one unproductive life, spent in and out of the welfare system, in and out of the penal system. The pain in Brian's life does not even come cheaply.

It is all too easy to dismiss the stories of Fatima and Brian as far-out tales from the front lines of Manhattan society. When we pick up the newspaper and read distressing articles about homeless or battered children, we sigh and feel badly for a moment or two, we then turn the page and look for some news that is more upbeat or mainstream. For, in rich nations, it is very tempting to handle bad news about children as strictly someone else's problem. Babies sometimes die, but generally these are poor, black babies. Families can become homeless, but the worst cases are somewhere else. Doesn't everyone know that New York City is a zoo? We see these as nasty, even painful, problems, but they don't belong to us. We try to convince ourselves: As long as we're not poor or black, as long as we don't live in the ghetto or the third world, our children are safe.

We are, of course, dead wrong.

Few families can escape the neglect that threatens to overwhelm children in the contemporary world. In the United Kingdom and the United States, more than a quarter of all babies are now born to single mothers, and many of these women find it impossible to provide shelter or safety for their children. In these countries a third of all children are forced to deal with the fallout from their parents' divorce, and almost half of these youngsters lose contact with their fathers, with predictable and often serious emotional consequences.

Kevin White is a case in point.

For our first chat, in June 1992, Kevin and I arranged to meet for coffee at Ann's Pantry, a small café in his home town of Ware. Just 40 miles north of London in the county of Hertfordshire, Ware is a placid, prosperous suburb surrounded by open wheat fields and gently rolling hills. At least on the surface, this green and pleasant land seems a world away from the violence and misery of New York City.

Kevin White looked quite incongruous among the elderly female shoppers chatting about a Women's Institute meeting as they fingered their pearls and patted their hairdos. It was 11 o'clock on a Friday morning, and most young people were at school or work, but Kevin had not been to school for a couple of weeks. June had been a bad month. Two ugly incidents — a bitter confrontation with an English teacher, a bloody fight with a much younger boy — had caused Kevin to drop out of sight for a while. He was not at all sure that he would ever go back to his secondary school.

In the summer of 1992, Kevin was just 15 but looked considerably older. Clad almost entirely in black, he had clearly given considerable thought to his outfit for our rendezvous at Ann's Pantry. A carefully ironed black turtle-neck and an expensive leather jacket were set off by black studded army boots and Ray-Ban aviator sun-glasses. But behind his shades this 'wannabe' warrior seemed quite nervous. Beads of sweat stood out on his forehead, and he cracked his finger joints as he struggled to find the words to tell me what had gone wrong with his life. Food seemed to help. Two hours into our conversation Kevin had consumed 12 orders of hot buttered toast. He said he found it soothing. He was, after all, just a kid.

Up until four years ago, Kevin had led a fairly normal life. He and his older brother and sister lived with their parents in a three-bedroom house on the outskirts of town. His Dad worked as a security guard, and his Mum had gone back to work when he was six, making circuit boards at a nearby electronics plant. Kevin sees this middle part of his childhood — between the age of 6 and 11 — as a golden period. "With both of them working we was (sic) beginning to get somewhere," he says wistfully. "We had money for summer holidays and we put in this new bathroom."

Two days before Christmas 1988, Kevin's father left his mother for another woman — a wealthy older woman, who at one time had employed his Dad. Kevin can't stand the new woman in his Dad's life. "She's a real snob, keeps on at me about my table manners and is always butting into conversations correcting the way I talk," he said, flushed with anger and hurt. Kevin learned to avoid his "stepmum" and has only been to his Dad's home twice in the last year.

Kevin's mother fell to pieces after his Dad left. "She used to come home from work and lock herself in the bathroom with a bottle of gin and pretty much cry herself through the evening," said Kevin, his face blank, his voice expressionless. "My older brother and sister moved out, and I was left to deal with her. I couldn't stand all of her crying, it made me mad. I yelled at her a lot, shoved her around a bit. It was bad." Kevin's voice was bleak, he cracked his finger joints with renewed vigour.

Just over a year ago, Kevin's mother finally pulled herself together and found a boyfriend.

"What is he like?" I asked. "Do you like him?"

Instead of answering, Kevin took off his aviator sun-glasses and wordlessly pointed to a fresh scar that ran, jagged and ugly, half an inch above his right eye.

"How did you get that?" I asked. A chill ran down my spine. I knew the answer.

"He laid into me last weekend and tried to rip my eyelid off," said Kevin nonchalantly, trying to look cool and uncaring. "You see he earns a living as a mercenary and is pretty violent."

"How did he get into that line of work?" I asked.

"Oh, I don't know," replied Kevin, "My Mum told me that he used to be in the army."

Kevin said the man was paid the equivalent of US$500 a day to fight in the Middle East. More recently, he was getting US$100 a day to take part in the war in former Yugoslavia, but came home because he thought the money wasn't enough.

"Says he can make more money driving a lorry," recalled Kevin.

"How long has he been living with you and your mother?"

Kevin cracked his finger joints some more before replying. "About a year," he sighed. "You know he just moved in too quick. I met him once, and before I knew it he was living in our house ordering my Mum around, using up all her attention. She is forever cooking special meals for him, ironing his uniforms, polishing his stupid military gear. She hardly knows I exist any more. And this bloke really doesn't like kids, he's got two of his own and hasn't bothered to see either of them in five years. Anyway, I soon figured I should look for my own girlfriend and that's how I ended up with Sam. She's great, and I spend most of my time with her now. I'm over at her house most evenings and weekends. Her Mom works shifts and Sam has the place to herself. Means we get up to all kinds of stuff; you know, sex, porno videos, that kind of thing." Kevin winked at me, an unpleasant, leering grimace.

I decided to change the subject. "How much homework do you do, Kevin?"

"Homework!" Kevin laughed loudly, as though the notion of doing homework was a great joke. "I don't do homework."

"Why not, Kevin?"

"I just don't have time."

"Hang on a second, what do you mean, you don't have time?" I said disbelievingly.

"Well, I get home from school about 4.30, then I eat my tea and get showered and changed — Sam's very particular — then I head off to Sam's and don't get home until about midnight."

"What do you do at Sam's?"

"Watch TV, fool around."

"How much TV?"

"Not much. Only four hours most nights."

"But, Kevin, you can't tell me you have no time for homework when you watch TV four hours every evening."

Kevin reluctantly saw my point. "I suppose I could, but there are so many distractions at Sam's house, and it isn't as though anyone else is doing homework."

"What do your teachers do when you don't turn in homework?"

"They give me detention, which I don't go to. Then they give me another detention for not going to detention, and I don't go again," Kevin grinned, delighted with himself. "Then they send a note home to my parents, and my Mum reads it and laughs. I mean there's no way teachers can make you do work at home unless your parents get in on the act. My Dad used to belt me if I got into trouble in school, but these days he's not on the scene."

Kevin has given little thought to his future. Mostly he wants to move in with Sam. "We're getting engaged when I turn 16 — in fact we are kind of engaged already — then in two years we'll get married," said Kevin proudly.

His ideas on the earning-a-living front are much more hazy. He used to think he would go into teaching — he always liked the idea of helping little kids — but that dream has receded as he became alienated from school. He now talks of doing something with motor bikes. Maybe he could become a rally driver, or get into the garage business. Working on high-performance bikes could be a turn-on.

The subject of bikes brought real animation to Kevin's face. He leaned forward eagerly: "Motor bikes are really my thing. There's nothing that beats tearing down some country road at 130 miles an hour, squealing around corners, brushing the ground with your knee." His eyes shone with excitement.

"Do you have your own bike?" I asked.

Kevin looked regretful. "There's no way I can afford the kind of bike I want, it would cost about three grand to buy and insure. Besides, I'm not old enough to ride yet — at least not legally. But I have this friend who — for a consideration — lets me 'borrow' his bike and his licence, and I've outridden the police a couple of times — just this last Sunday, riding down the A10, I lost them in the fog. I must have been doing 120."

"In the fog?" I was appalled at the notion of this disturbed 15-year-old, in the fog, loose on a high-performance bike, jeopardizing his own and everyone else's safety. There were grounds for my anxiety. Two of Kevin's schoolmates had recently been killed on motor bikes, and one of these accidents involved an elderly pedestrian who subsequently died.

The fact is youngsters like Fatima, Brian and Kevin are unlikely to become productive law-abiding citizens. Deprivation and rejection — whether in mid-town Manhattan or the English home counties — yield a harvest of failure and violence. If we take good care of our children they will add to the productive capability of an economy; if we fail to look after our children they will drag a nation down. To quote the words of late US President Lyndon B. Johnson, "Ignorance, ill health, personality disorders — these are destructions often contracted in childhood; afflictions that will cripple the man and damage the nation."

Sweden's liberal parenting leave policies give families the needed time to spend with their children. Available to both men and women, parenting leave encourages fathers to be more involved in child-rearing.

Some successful initiatives

Prenatal and postnatal care: Netherlands

Perinatal care, consisting of the services provided for mothers before, during and immediately after childbirth, is particularly effective and comprehensive in the Netherlands. Central to this country's policies is the principle that giving birth is a natural process rather than an affliction and that it should, if possible, be based at home. From this principle has grown 'maternity home care', a support service that combines medical care with practical assistance to the mother and her family, run by the Dutch Cross Society.[55]

Current maternity care practice in the Netherlands developed in response to a high perinatal death rate of about 35 per cent at the turn of the century. Early attempts to train professionals to assist in home deliveries were inadequate and disorganized, and resulted in the creation of a government-appointed maternity care committee, which published a landmark report in 1943. The report led to significant changes, the most important being the training of maternity care assistants in centres run by fully qualified specialist nurses. At the high point, there were 16 such schools.

In recent years, budget cuts, growing pressure from the medical establishment for care assistants to receive broader training, and declining birth rates have led to the closing of these residential schools. In their place are two new training courses: one offered by secondary schools; the other, a three-year full-time course that qualifies care assistants in a range of related fields, including perinatal care, family welfare, and care for the elderly and the physically handicapped.

The Dutch Cross Society admits that the move away from specialists has meant some small loss in the quality of care. Nevertheless, the rights and benefits available to pregnant women in the Netherlands are still impressive. At the heart of the system are the midwife, a major player in maternity care throughout Europe, and the home visit, a source of preventive care and parent education.[56]

The system operates in the following way: A pregnant woman first contacts her general practitioner and then decides whether to continue with the doctor or transfer to a privately practising midwife, who in the Netherlands is office- rather than hospital-based. High-risk pregnancies are referred to an obstetrician, which is one of the main reasons why home delivery is regarded as a safe alternative and is officially endorsed. (The health insurance fund will not pay for care by an obstetrician unless medical indications require it.)

Prenatal care provided by the Cross Society encompasses health care education in group sessions, gymnastic classes and home visits. Prenatal health education groups, open to women and their partners, are often organized in collaboration with midwives. They concentrate on providing information on such subjects as the growth and development of the foetus, diet, labour and caring for the new baby. The sessions operate as support networks for expectant mothers and complement home visits, which offer guidance of a more individual kind. Home visits aim to prepare parents for the psychological impact of birth and the lifestyle changes it entails, as well as to inform them of the services available, from the loan of nursing equipment to the health screening of babies and children up to the age of four. A 1987 survey indicated that pregnant women in the Netherlands are visited at least once before birth, and postnatal visits are made on a daily basis for 8 hours a day, up to a maximum of 10 days.[57]

The Cross Society's prenatal gymnastic classes are popular and over-subscribed. In 1988, 45 per cent of all pregnant women in the Netherlands took part. Over the course of 8 to 10 sessions, a physiotherapist prepares women for the rigours of delivery, emphasizing a woman's active role in what happens to her and teaching breathing and relaxation techniques that will help diminish her fear and stress. Classes aimed at restoring the functions of a woman's body after birth are also offered by many of the local branches of the Cross Society, but not all, because postnatal gymnastic classes are not paid for by the health insurance fund.

A surge in the popularity of hospital births during the 1970s — 57 per cent of births took place at home in 1970, but by 1989 the figure had dropped to 33 per cent — led to the establishment of the 'golden mean' of polyclinic delivery. This means that a woman gives birth in hospital, without a formal admission and usually under the supervision of a midwife. If all goes well, she returns home after 36 hours (or even 24 hours), unless there is a medical reason for her to remain in hospital, such as a premature or Caesarean birth. The mother then receives a level of maternity home care determined by her choice and financial considerations, since families have to pay 300 guilders (approximately US$150) for 8 to 10 days of full home care. Without the benefit of Cross Society membership or private insurance, costs can be much higher.

Contributions, at an average of less than US$20 per year, cover one fifth of the cost of most of the Society's services; the rest comes from the insurance moneys levied by the tax authorities. The exception is maternity care, which to a large extent is financed through the national health care insurance fund. The fund provides 70 per cent of the Dutch population with free care by general practitioners and specialists including midwives, free dentistry, free medication and nursing care in either general or psychiatric hospitals. Contributions are mandatory for workers below a certain income level (about US$21,000). The fund provides not only for employees paying the premium but also for their families, non-working students and the disabled. The remaining 30 per cent of the population holds private medical insurance policies.

On a home visit, a maternity care assistant typically checks on the baby's physical condition, gives practical help with breastfeeding, advises on birth control, looks after older siblings and helps out with household chores such as shopping, cleaning and cooking. One mother may decide she needs maternity care visits for only one hour twice a day, while another may opt for the full eight hours. Whatever level is chosen, the new mother is also visited by the midwife or general practitioner who attended her delivery. He or she offers counselling on infant care and follows up on the mother's health and physical condition after the birth. At four weeks, 90 per cent of new babies attend a well-baby clinic, one of 3,000 organized and run by the Cross Society. During the first year of life, a baby attends a clinic an average of 10 times.

The maternity care provided in the Netherlands by the Dutch Cross Society seems hard to fault. It is sensitive to the needs of the new mother and has the additional advantage of being low cost, because expensive obstetricians are used only in complicated or risky cases. However, high-quality home care accessible to all is an ideal that has been affected by recent budget cuts. The provision of 10 days of home care is no longer automatic but "tailored to the individual situation of the family."[58] Since 1987, a 10 per cent cut-back in mandated services has been accompanied by calls for a greater reliance on the private market. Recently, the Minister of Public Health suggested that the maximum period of home care should be cut to five days.[59]

Despite these worrisome developments, perinatal care in the Netherlands still attains an extremely high standard. Strictly in terms of health, Dutch babies do very well (the neonatal mortality rate in 1989 was 3.8 per 1,000 live births, which places it at the low end of the European scale). What's more, the system of home births and/or care at home after delivery underpins and supports the family in the critical post-partum period, and in so doing plays a role in preventing the development of a broad range of problems.

Experts at the Dutch Cross Society are convinced that a qualified maternity care assistant operating in a home can both detect incipient problems and help resolve them in areas as diverse as dental care, birth control and child abuse. Especially with young children, prevention is so much better than cure, and home visits are a good example of how government can help create the conditions that allow mothers and babies to flourish, rather than wait until families are already in crisis and offer damage control.

Prevention is so much better than cure, and home visits are a good example of how government can help create the conditions that allow mothers and babies to flourish, rather than wait until families are already in crisis and offer damage control.

Parenting leave: Sweden

Sweden has one of the most liberal parenting leave policies in the developed world. New parents are now entitled to 450 days (approximately 15 months) of paid leave when a child is born. Not only is Swedish policy particularly generous in the amount of time given to new parents, it also avoids the discriminatory aspects of the more standard maternity leave policies. Because parenting leave is equally available to both men and women, it is hard for employers to use it as an excuse to fail to hire or promote mothers.

Parenting leave is the most important component of parental insurance, which is part of Sweden's social insurance system and comes under

A Swedish father comes home from shopping with his two children. Sexual stereotypes are breaking down under the Government's liberal parenting leave plans.

the National Insurance Act. The first maternity benefits were established in 1937 and combined a cash grant with a job guarantee. In 1974, Sweden shifted from maternity to 'parenting benefits', creating a six-month paid parenting leave for both mothers and fathers. This was extended to 360 days in 1980 and to 450 days in 1989. Both natural and adopted children are included. Parenting leave has gradually expanded as increasing numbers of Swedish women have entered the labour force — today, 80 per cent of all Swedish women with children under the age of seven are employed full or part time.[60]

Parenting leave can be used entirely by one parent or shared between them. In the latter case, parents decide how to divide up the 450 days, since only one can receive compensation at a time. Leave can be used to stay at home full time or it can be combined with part-time employment, in which case the parent receives a combination of salary from the employer and benefits from the insurance system. The 450 days can be taken until a child's eighth birthday. For the first 360 days, parenting leave is paid at 90 per cent of the parent's gross income. For the final 90 days, a fixed reimbursement rate of 60 kronor (about US$8) per day is paid. An extension of this benefit to 18 months at 90 per cent of income for the entire period was scheduled to go into effect in 1991, but has been abandoned.

When parenting leave was first introduced in 1974, only 3 per cent of fathers took advantage of it; in 1986, 23 per cent of those drawing this benefit were fathers; in 1990, 26.1 per cent were.[61] It seems that if a government creates a parenting entitlement that is both generous and available to both sexes, sexual stereotypes do begin to break down. A quarter of Swedish employers are now tolerating, even supporting, 'daddies on velvet.'

Sweden is one of only two countries to have established male rights to parenting leave on a large scale. Interestingly, the other country is Australia. As of July 1990, Australian male employees with 12 months of continuous service are entitled to 52 weeks of unpaid leave in order to become the primary caregiver of a newborn child. Because this is unpaid leave, no one expects the 'take up' rate to be very significant. However, this new entitlement does advance the cause of equal parenting.[62]

A second component of the parental insurance system in Sweden is the '10-day benefit', which entitles the father to a special paid leave of up to 10 days for childbirth. A father is entitled to this leave even if the mother is receiving parenting benefits for the same child at the same time. In 1990, the benefit was used by 109,000 men, 86 per cent of all fathers of children born that year.

A third component is the 'temporary child-care benefit', which reimburses parents for the loss of income involved when one of them stays home to care for a child — their own child or an adopted child, foster child or stepchild. This benefit is payable for up to 90 days per child annually and occasionally can be extended to 120 days. Situations qualifying for the benefit are: when a child falls ill; when the person who looks after the child falls ill; when one parent needs to look after a child at home while the other parent takes another child to a doctor or hospital. Compensation is 80 per cent of income for the first 14 days and 90 per cent thereafter.

A fourth component of parental insurance is a 'contact days benefit', which entitles parents with children between the ages of 4 and 12 to take two days off work per child each year to visit the child's preschool, leisure centre or school. Parents are fully compensated for loss of income incurred on these days. In 1990, contact days were paid for 29 per cent of all children in the 4- to 12-year-old age group.

And last, a 'pregnancy cash benefit' is payable to expectant mothers who are unable to continue with their normal tasks during the latter stages of pregnancy and who cannot be assigned more suitable work. The pregnancy cash benefit is paid at the same rate as the parenting

Over the last several decades Swedish social benefits have gone hand in hand with successful economic growth.

benefit and is payable for a maximum of 50 days during the last two months of pregnancy. In 1990 the average number of benefit days per pregnancy was 39.[63]

To non-Swedish eyes, this list of parental benefits seems astonishingly generous, even profligate, and yet government officials justify the policies on economic grounds. "Swedish employers want productive employees," according to Bo Adolfsson, labour counsellor at the Swedish Embassy in Washington, D.C. "Women in America go back to work, and they aren't good on the job because they are worried about their child. Turnover is high. The main reason is not low wages but, more likely, bad child care."[64]

It is important to remember that over the last several decades Swedish social benefits have gone hand in hand with successful economic growth: GNP per capita is now US$25,490, the third highest in the world, and above the per capita figure for the United States, which stands at US$22,560.[65]

Child care: France

France has the most comprehensive child-care system in Western Europe. Responsibility for the provision and control of child-care services is shared between the Ministry of Social Affairs, which works through local authorities and covers nursery and child-minding facilities for children under the age of three, and the Ministry of Education, which provides preschools for children of ages two to six. Today, almost every French child between the age of three and six and nearly half of all children aged two to two and a half attend some form of preschool. Preschool care, while not compulsory, not only supports maternal employment, but also provides a vital first step in the socialization and development of French children.[66]

For reasons ranging from increased female employment to trade union pressure and pronatalist sentiment, child care in France has been defined for some time as a public responsibility. Increasingly, extended periods of maternity, paternity or child-care leave mean that many of the youngest children in France are in their parents' care. Nevertheless, 33 per cent of those under age three are in day care, including 10 per cent of those under two. Most provision for this type of care is made by local authorities, or is otherwise publicly funded.[67]

France boasts a long tradition of out-of-home care. As early as 1771, Jean-Frédéric Oberlin, a Protestant pastor, set up infant schools in remote villages in the Alsace mountains so women could work in the local timber industry. In the 19th century, crèches were established by philanthropic agencies with the aim of reducing poverty and infant mortality among the working classes by freeing mothers to work outside the home. In the postwar era, crèches and *écoles maternelles* (publicly funded preschools), have become an integral part of the French social security and family support system. Once considered welfare institutions for the poor, crèches are now in great demand by middle-class working parents. Today, all

crèches take children up to the age of three and are partially subsidized by the State.

Crèches collectives are essentially crèches that offer full-day care, 8 to 12 hours per day for children under three. Places are restricted to children of working mothers. Eighty per cent of the *crèches collectives* are for use by residents of a particular neighbourhood; the remaining 20 per cent are attached to workplaces — mainly hospitals — with opening hours designed to suit employee needs. The average facility accommodates 50 children, divided into either two or three age groups. Older children are organized in groups of 10 to 12 with an *éducatrice* (instructor) for part of the day. In France, 85,000 children (4 per cent of the under-threes) attend *crèches collectives*. About 6,600 children are looked after in *mini-crèches*, which take fewer than 16 children and are usually situated in apartments or houses.

The fees for *crèches collectives* are income-related and range from 15 to 85 French francs (about US$3 to US$17) per day. In 1987, 26 per cent of the cost was borne by parents. The remaining costs were divided between local authorities (54 per cent) and regional family allowance offices known as *caisses des allocations familiales* (20 per cent).[68] These offices, funded by employee contributions, were originally set up to give cash benefits to needy families with children, but since the 1970s they have

Children form a circle under adult supervision in a French école maternelle, *where priority is given to children of working parents.*

subsidized child-care services, thus allowing local authorities to expand services for children under age three. (Expenditure by the *caisses* rose by 41 per cent between 1984 and 1987.) Their objective is to increase the quality as well as the quantity of child-care places, both by reducing the size of nursery classes and by providing a greater diversity of services. Their recommendation is that child-care costs should be around 12 per cent of family income.

With the number of working mothers growing rapidly, the few available crèches have long waiting lists. Large cities such as Paris, Lyons, Marseilles and Orleans have more crèches than poor rural districts. For example, nearly half of all available places in nurseries are in the Ile-de-France region around Paris, although this area has less than one fifth of the French population.

Crèches familiales (family day care) is based in the home of an *assistante maternelle* or *nourrice*, both child-minders, and staffed by caregivers who are supposed to be registered and approved by the authorities, but frequently operate without a licence. Each caregiver takes responsibility for a maximum of three children, including her own. The public agency that enrols and supervises the *assistantes maternelles* is headed by a paediatric nurse, who organizes medical examinations and collects parental fees, which are income-related; pays caregivers; and provides equipment and assistance. A statute passed in 1977 gave the *assistantes maternelles* legal entitlements including rights to a minimum

Going to the park: French preschools help children develop confidence, giving them an advantage in later schooling.

wage, social insurance and paid holidays; but many still resist registration because it makes them liable for income taxes.

A *crèche familiale* costs less than a *crèche collective* because in the former, the children are taken care of in a private home, where operating costs are typically about 30 per cent lower than those of centre care. In 1987, there were 46,400 places in this type of day care (2 per cent of the children under age three); 38 per cent of the costs were paid by parents, 42 per cent by local authorities and 20 per cent by the *caisses*.

Haltes-garderies are part-time nurseries offering 41,400 places for children up to the age of six, though most attending are under three. Originally intended to care a few hours each week for the children of non-working mothers while they went shopping or pursued other interests, *haltes-garderies* are gradually turning into part-time mini-nurseries, in response to the growth in part-time employment.

And finally, there are private child-minders — about 138,000 who are registered care for approximately 200,000 children under age three (about 9 per cent of the total). An additional number who are unregistered look after at least 130,000 children under age three. The latter, like the *assistantes maternelles* above, resist registration because once their activity becomes official, they are liable for income taxes. However, in 1981, France introduced tax relief on day-care expenses incurred by families, and this has encouraged registration.

The French *écoles maternelles* (publicly funded preschools), were established in the 1950s. Today, the schools are so popular that places for two-year-olds are invariably oversubscribed. Preference is given to children of working parents. There is more space available for older children, however: Only 60 per cent of mothers with children aged three to five are in the workforce, yet more than 95 per cent of children in this age group participate in the preschool system. Hours are generally from 8.30 a.m. to 4.30 p.m. But outside school hours, when working parents need a complementary child-care facility, *service périscolaire* is available in recreation centres that are generally attached to the preschools and open at 7.30 a.m. and close at 6.30 p.m. The *école maternelle* itself usually adjoins a primary school, but has its own director and exists as a separate entity.

There are three levels within preschool: ages two to three and a half (called *les tout-petits*, the little ones); ages three and a half to five (*les moyens*, the middle ones); and ages five to six (*les grands*, the big ones). Emphasis is placed on encouraging children to develop confidence and self-esteem, as well as on learning how to learn, in preparation for primary school. Research has found that French children who do not attend the preschool programme are likely to be at a disadvantage when they begin regular school.

From 20 to 30 per cent of the cost of the *écoles maternelles* is paid for by the central Government, the rest is underwritten by the local authorities. Tuition is free, but parents do pay income-related fees for meals, before- and after-school care, and Wednesday afternoon programmes (when French schools are closed).

Throughout the 1980s, there was a steady increase in the provision of publicly funded child care in France. The rise in the proportion of young

In France ... recent Governments have all recognized that proper preschool care and education are an investment in the nation's future citizens.

mothers joining the labour force has undoubtedly been a major spur to the development of such an impressive system, but that is only part of the story. Recent Governments have all recognized that proper preschool care and education are an investment in the nation's future citizens.[69] Olga Baudelot of the National Institute of Pedagogical Research in Paris makes a cost-benefit case for publicly funded day care. "Child care," she says, "has freed a million women to work and allowed 500,000 others to make a living out of child care. These women are consumers and taxpayers."[70]

Child care and child rights: United Kingdom

Interestingly, the United Kingdom, a nation that publicly funds a mere 2 per cent of its day-care places, has produced some of the most fine-grained research on the costs and benefits of child care. Two reports, both published in 1991, demonstrate convincingly that creating a comprehensive child-care service in the United Kingdom would boost the economy as well as strengthen the financial and educational circumstances of British children.

In one of the reports, for the National Children's Bureau, Sally Holtermann estimated that it would cost £550 million (£1 = US$1.50, 1 September 1993) to improve and expand existing child-care services sufficiently to accommodate an extra 2 million children. That would allow the percentage of women with a child under 11 who are in paid employment to rise to 70 per cent, from 50 per cent in 1989. One and a quarter million 'extra' parents at work would boost the national economy by approximately £12 billion. In the Holtermann study, the positive effects of expanded subsidized child care were wide-ranging and included the creation of about 350,000 jobs in child care and the lifting out of poverty of 500,000 children in families currently dependent on income support.[71]

The second study, published by the Institute of Public Policy Research, has estimated that up to half a million children could be lifted out of poverty if high-quality, affordable child-care services freed their mothers to work.[72] In this study, the direct rate of return to the Government for moneys invested in child care ranges from 5 per cent to 51 per cent over a 13-year period, depending on how intensively parents use child-care services. And the social rate of return — which includes the economic gain for the household (enhanced earnings) as well as flowback to the Government (taxes) — ranges from 24 per cent to 84 per cent.

Recently, children's rights in the United Kingdom have also gained attention through the Children Act (1989), which came into force on 14 October 1991. The Act has been described by the Lord Chancellor, Lord Mackay, as "the most comprehensive and far-reaching reform of child law... in living memory."[73] That may be an exaggerated claim for an Act that has yet to have much effect on children, but many of its limitations are due to funding shortfalls. In the sphere of principle, the Children Act is on the cutting edge of attempts to make legal systems more responsive to the

needs and rights of children.

A systematic review of laws relating to children was launched in the 1980s after a House of Commons Select Committee report described existing legislation as complex, confusing and unsatisfactory.[74] The Act was also, in part, a response to the debate following inquiries into the child-abuse related deaths of three children: Jasmine Beckford (1985), Tyra Henry (1987) and Kimberly Carlisle (1987). The inquiry into Kimberly's death concluded that the law had failed the social workers in their primary task of protecting the child because no legal mechanism had been available to allow them access to her or to ensure that she had a medical examination.[75]

The Act brings together legislation from both private and public law. Items covered under private law include, for example, disputes between divorcing parents about the future of their children. Public law, on the other hand, deals with public policy issues such as the duties and powers of local authorities. A central thrust of the Act is that the welfare of children should be 'paramount' in all of these legal contexts. A basic recommendation is that children should be brought up within their own families whenever possible. They should be taken into care only when it is absolutely necessary, because the best place for a child to be is in his or her own home.

A young boy in the UK lives in an area where many flats are boarded up as unfit for habitation. A recent study estimates that half a million children could be lifted out of poverty if affordable day care freed mothers to work.

The language of the Act represents a distinct change of emphasis. The words 'parents' rights', 'custody' and 'access' are replaced by 'parental responsibility', 'partnership' and 'contact'. Parents still have rights, but the emphasis now is on responsibilities — how a parent can best safeguard the well-being of a child, how best to take into account a child's wishes and needs. In fact, the Act attempts to give new priority to children in divorce proceedings, stating that "never again will parents in separation or divorce battles be able to lay claim to their children as if they were property."

The Children Act is also a step forward for fathers, as it encourages divorcing parents to negotiate shared responsibility for their children. At least for married individuals, parental responsibility is now for life. (In the case of unmarried fathers, parental responsibility is not automatic, but can be acquired if the mother agrees, or the court rules, that he should have it.)

Should parents be unable to agree on how to distribute parental responsibility in the wake of separation or divorce, the court can pass a variety of Section 8 orders. Examples are a Resident Order, which stipulates where the child should live; a Contact Order, which may require the parent with whom the child is living to allow telephone calls, visits and overnight stays with the other parent; or a Specific Issue Order, which settles a particular area of dispute, such as the choice of a school. Indeed, anyone concerned about the welfare of the child may apply for a Section 8 order. Grandparents, for example, may contest an adoption order and ask that the child come to live with them.

Many of these new regulations need adequate funding if they are to be properly implemented. For example, budget cuts in the 1980s undermined a non-custodial parent's financial responsibility for a child by reducing the number of social security staff devoted to collecting child maintenance. The result was 9 per cent less child maintenance collected from 1988 to 1989 than from 1981 to 1982.

Regulations under the Children Act that mandate a certain level of local authorities' services have already run into severe funding constraints. These new regulations cover disparate matters, from the rules governing private foster-care arrangements, to the registration and inspection of child-minders and children's homes.

Many professionals believe that the resources necessary to implement the Act — whether for regulation, inspection or training — are simply not there. For example, they argue that the $3.5 million available nationally for training is nowhere near enough. Brian Doughty, head of Strategy and Development for the region of North Tyneside, has complained that the resources are totally inadequate and have to be "massively topped up from the local authorities' existing budgets. If central government really wishes to promote the welfare of young children and ensure they have access to the range of services of the Children Act ... they should ensure adequate finances are made available."[76] The Association of County Councils estimates that implementation of the Act will cost as much as $150 million nationwide.

Clearly, many of the Act's good intentions will come to naught without proper funding, and they might even have undesirable consequences. One example is the proposal to expand the registration scheme for child-minders to include all those caring for children up to the age of eight. (Current provision is limited to under the age of five.) Local authorities must not only re-register and inspect every child-minder already on their books — more than 100,000 in England and Wales — but they must also register and inspect new child-minders and check them for appropriate attitudes to children's cultural, religious and dietary needs.

Most local authorities despair of meeting the Act's demands. For example, in the town of Sutton, insufficient resources and staff have created such a backlog that the authority is unable to register any new child-minders at all, leaving the field wide open for people to work outside the law — the very danger the Act was designed to combat. Another problem concerns high fees. Registration fees of £100 and inspection fees of £75 for nurseries and playgroups may signal the end for small, informal programmes that survive on a shoestring budget.

The Children Act sets high standards for the United Kingdom, and yet at present, the Government seems unwilling to provide the resources necessary to meet those standards.[77] Children with special needs are a case in point. The Act requires local authorities to provide support for disabled children and latchkey children. But without central government support, how can financially strapped local authorities provide after-school programmes or special schooling? This paradoxical situation compromises many of the recent reforms in education and health care, which are bound to fail because there has been no commensurate increase in the size of budgets. Indeed, in some critical areas — such as industrial training — budgets are actually shrinking.

Family allowances: Belgium

Family allowances, sometimes referred to as 'child benefits' or 'child allowances', were first adopted in Europe in the 1930s to combat falling birth rates and to supplement family income at a time of high unemployment. Initially financed by an employer payroll tax, many European countries gradually moved towards family allowances financed from general government revenue. In the 1950s and 1960s, these allowances were permitted to erode in value, but this trend was reversed in the late 1960s, when governments became concerned once more about poverty in large families and the rise in the number of single-parent families. Then, in the late 1970s, the allowances declined again. In most European countries, family allowances have dwindled over time as a proportion of family income, although they remain important to low-income families.

There are striking similarities in the pattern of benefits. Throughout the European Community, member States pay family allowances through their social security systems, targeting the mother as the recipient of the

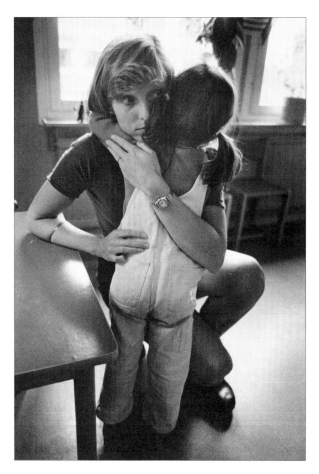

A trained day-care assistant provides crucial emotional support to a young child.

benefit. Most pay more for larger families and older children, and design the family allowance as a universal rather than a means-tested benefit.

In a recent report using data from 1990, Belgium emerged as having the most generous system of family allowances in Europe administered by a powerful Ministry for the Family.

As is the case in some other European countries, family support policy in Belgium was once tied to a strong pronatalist approach, designed to encourage families to have more children. Thus, the payment gradient is steep — the rate for the third child being three times the rate for the first. (Rates range from approximately US$70 a month for the first child to US$220 a month for the third child.) The rate per child also rises with the age of the child. The Belgian family allowance is not means-tested and is payable until the child reaches the age of 18 or completes full-time education. In practice, many families collect until age 25.

In Belgium, the family allowance is referred to as an 'indirect wage', and it is a significant source of economic security for families. However, it has not been immune to the spending cuts of the 1980s. The family allowance as a percentage of a family's after-tax income diminished from 3.8 per cent in 1980 to 3.2 per cent in 1986. In recent years, the allowance has lagged behind the rise in wages, and as a result, families with children have fallen behind.

There are calls in Belgium for the child, rather than the mother or the father, to become the 'entitled person'. (This is often seen as a solution to problems raised by changing caretakers, which occurs with divorce or re-marriage.) There are also new pressures for higher family allowances, coming from Belgium's strong 'family movement', which is conservative in orientation. The movement, which has particular currency among the Catholic population, stresses that higher allowances would enable more women to stay out of the paid labour force, thus preserving the traditional division of labour between men and women.

Outside the European Community, the leading country in family allowances is Sweden, which adopted them in the 1930s. Sweden's family benefits were not inspired by pronatalism. Rather, they have aimed at redistributing resources in favour of families with children and at providing better employment opportunities for women with children.

A European Community survey in 1990 found that the level of family allowance was not a key factor in influencing a person's decision to have a baby; it ranked seventh on the list. Economic prospects, availability of housing, the existence of child-care facilities and the strength of the marital relationship were all more important determinants. It seems that pronatalism is no longer the dominant force behind this benefit. Instead, family allowances are part of a general commitment in Europe to family and child welfare, a commitment that has been sadly lacking in other rich nations.

Divorce reform: France, Sweden, United States (Wisconsin)

The adverse consequences of divorce for children seem to be particularly severe in the United States and the United Kingdom. This is because, more so than in other countries, reformist energies in the 1970s and 1980s were directed towards maximizing adult rights to freedom and equality rather than towards providing a safety net for children. As Mary Ann Glendon has noted, those Anglo-American countries are unique in the degree to which they have accepted no-fault, no-responsibility divorce, and in their "relative carelessness about assuring either public or private responsibility" for children.[78]

The divorce reform movement produced two models in Western Europe: a 'traditional' model (found in France and Italy), which emphasizes private responsibility and the financial obligation of the former provider; and a 'Nordic' model (in Sweden and Norway), which relies on elaborate programmes of public support for single parents with children.

France liberalized its divorce laws in 1975, but was careful to continue to protect the economic interests of women and children. All assets acquired during marriage are now divided equally, and the spouse with the higher income (nearly always the husband) is required to make payments to the other "to compensate ... for the disparity which the disruption of the marriage creates in the conditions of their respective lives."[79] In addition, child support awards are generous, and if the non-custodial parent fails to pay, the State rather than the custodial parent absorbs the risk. This means that if there is a default in child support payments, all the custodial parent needs to do is apply to a State agency. The agency then tries to collect from the non-custodial parent, but in the meantime it advances the amount of child support owed, up to a limit set by law.

Cases of unilateral no-fault divorce are governed by a particularly strict set of rules in France. The plaintiff must not only wait six years for a divorce, but "remains completely bound to the duty" of supporting his wife and children in their current lifestyle.[80] All of these safeguards help ensure a reasonable standard of living for children in the case of divorce.

Sweden protects its children in other ways. Like France, child support is guaranteed by the State, but instead of relying on alimony or other support for a divorced spouse to maintain a certain standard of living, child support is backed with "the most comprehensive and gener-

Reformist energies in the 1970s and 1980s were directed towards maximizing adult rights to freedom and equality rather than towards providing a safety net for children.

ous package of benefits for one-parent families in the world."[81] As one divorcee explained, "Everyone knows that divorced parents need more money and more social support because of the additional pressures involved in raising children as a single parent ... So, as soon as I got divorced my income went up: Both the local and national Government increased maternal benefits, my tax rate dropped drastically ... It also helped to have the possibility of 24-hour day care."[82]

In the United States, a few states are beginning to move in a 'European' direction in order to better protect the interests of children. For example, in 1987, the state of Wisconsin drew up guidelines for child support awards. The new standards are generous — 17 per cent of the non-custodial parent's income for one child, rising to 35 per cent for five or more children — and they have dramatically increased the monetary value of child support. At the same time, Wisconsin instituted a system of routinely withholding child support from the salaries of non-custodial parents, and this has brought delinquency rates down. The net result: Custodial parents are granted much larger child support awards, and the awards are much more likely to be paid.

Wisconsin has also increased the coverage of child support awards by treating never-married fathers (where it is possible to establish paternity) in exactly the same way as divorced fathers, using identical guidelines and collection procedures. State officials estimate that eventually 40 per cent of never-married fathers will be forced to contribute child support.[83]

A powerful feature of the Wisconsin initiative is that it sets a 'socially assured minimum benefit'; if the non-custodial parent's child support payments are lower than this benefit, the state steps in and pays the difference.

But is the Wisconsin model enough? Easing financial hardship is an extremely important goal, but it does not heal the psychological wounds of divorce. The research evidence seems overwhelming: No matter how prosperous their environment, abandoned children still yearn for their fathers and underperform in school.

If governments decide that a father's presence, as well as a father's salary, is important to the welfare of children, policy-making becomes a great deal more complicated. The State can no longer 'fix' the divorce problem by simply producing bigger and more reliable child support payments. It needs to venture into more difficult territory. Bringing divorce rates down and, when the breakup cannot be avoided, maximizing contact between the non-custodial parent and the child both become targets for legislation.

Despite the United Kingdom's dismal performance on the child support front (with payments actually shrinking in the 1980s), the United Kingdom is taking these non-economic issues seriously. Early in 1992, Lord Mackay, the Lord Chancellor, rejected proposals made by the Law Commission to further liberalize the divorce laws on the grounds that they would undermine families with children even more. Lord Mackay has spoken eloquently about the problem: "The Law Commission did not recognize sufficiently clearly the need to strengthen the institution of marriage."[84] It seems likely that the United Kingdom will move towards making divorce more difficult. Lord Mackay is thought to favour a longer waiting period for contested divorces, along the lines of French practice.

Family-friendly workplaces: United Kingdom, United States

Over the last decade the United Kingdom and the United States have seen a fivefold increase in the number of companies offering a package of family-friendly benefits to working mothers and fathers. This dramatic development has been prompted by two powerful trends: a massive deterioration in the life circumstances of children and the looming skill shortages of the 1990s.

Throughout the advanced industrial world, corporate executives warn of a "widening skills gap."[85] In Australia and Canada, business leaders worry about an "employment crisis,"[86] while in the United States analysts talk about a "monumental mismatch" between jobs and the ability of workers to do them.[87] Across countries and across economic sectors, corporations are caught in a bind as far as human resources are concerned and face growing competition for a limited, skilled workforce.

A mother and son converse as she drops him off at school on her way to work in Philadelphia. The rapid shift of mothers into the paid workforce has considerably shortened the time they can spend with their children.

The human capital deficit seems to be considerably worse in the United Kingdom and the United States than elsewhere, because in those countries the emerging shortfall in skills has been exacerbated by public policy. While most other nations have enacted elaborate family benefits, in the United Kingdom and the United States, public policy has tended to undermine rather than bolster fragile family structures, leaving to the private sector the unenviable task of picking up the pieces. This works best when companies can prove that family-friendly workplaces are good for the bottom line.

In the United States, an impressive body of evidence now exists to show that in-house programmes of family support can improve corporate profitability. One large national survey reports the following 'payoffs' to family benefits: improved recruitment (cited by 85 per cent of respondents), reduced turnover (65 per cent), reduced absenteeism (53 per cent), increased productivity (49 per cent) and enhanced company image (85 per cent).[88] Over the last three years, several high profile companies, including investment banking firms, such as Goldman Sachs and Bankers

47

Trust, have sponsored on-site day-care centres in their efforts to capture these 'payoffs'.

A few companies have analysed in detail the costs and benefits of specific family support policies. For example, the Union Bank in California has shown that on-site child care dramatically reduces labour turnover among working mothers (from 9.5 per cent to 2.2 per cent a year), producing significant savings for the company.[89] Honeywell, a computer manufacturer based in Minnesota, has introduced a sick-child-care programme that has cut back on absenteeism and reduced labour costs.[90] And Merck, the large pharmaceutical firm, has demonstrated impressive returns from its parenting leave policy. The price tag attached to replacing an employee at Merck is US$50,000. By permitting a new parent to take a generous six-month child-care leave (cost: US$38,000, which includes partial pay, benefits and other indirect costs), the company succeeds in retaining almost all of its new mothers, thereby achieving a net savings of US$12,000 per employee.[91]

J. Douglas Phillips, Senior Director of Corporate Planning at Merck, stresses the large cost savings inherent in bringing attrition rates down. In an analysis of turnover costs — duplicated in other companies with similar results — he showed that turnover costs average 1.5 times annual salary costs. According to Phillips, few companies are aware of how expensive it is to replace workers, but in most firms, "avoiding turnover for just a few employees will yield excellent paybacks."[92] His research shows that while other programmes are capable of reducing attrition rates, parenting leave and other family benefits have the greatest impact on turnover. He believes that Merck's family support package helps account for the company's low annual turnover of 5.5 per cent, compared with the American average of more than 12 per cent.

The United Kingdom shares with the United States a dearth of public policies on the family support front and, as is the case in the United States, British companies have been drawn in to fill the vacuum. For example, the Midland Bank has set up 300 on-site day-care centres in an attempt to stop large numbers of women from permanently leaving the bank after they have children. According to one senior executive at Midland, "The value of the women who leave is incalculable because of their experience and training."[93]

Company-sponsored day care or parenting leave is obviously much less needed in countries where there are well-developed public policies in these areas. In France, for example, there are relatively few unmet needs on the child-care front, and therefore little incentive for corporations to step in with their own programmes.

It is important to emphasize that working parents need time as well as benefits. Companies at the cutting edge of family policy have found flexible hours, compressed work weeks, part-time work with benefits, job-sharing, career-sequencing, extended parenting leave and home-based employment opportunities particularly popular among employees.

Corporations as different as IBM (200,000 employees) and NCNB Corporation, a Charlotte, North Carolina-based bank holding company (13,000 employees), have found it possible to create a more fluid, less rigid workplace that gives workers with family responsibilities significant discretion over how they structure their careers, how many hours they work each week, and when and where work is performed. For example, IBM employees can now take a three-year break from full-time employment, with an option of working part time in the second and third year, to take care of young children or elderly relatives. With the exception of the part-time component, this 'career break' is unpaid, but health and retirement benefits continue while workers are on leave, and IBM guarantees a full-time job at the end of the three years.

This 'gift of time' has proved immensely popular and has remained in place as a key employee benefit, despite the cut-backs at IBM over the last year.[94] In hard-pressed dual-income American households, many parents are desperate for such relief on the scheduling front.

Young girls in a school in Wales learn in two languages. While schools can do more to prepare children for future job markets, the home background and parental support play an even greater role in student achievement.

Whither in the future?

In the first two chapters of this publication, we explored the depth and scope of child neglect in the Anglo-American world. We now understand the plight of poor children in rich nations. Homelessness and ill-health are the lot of hundreds of thousands of youngsters in advanced industrial countries. We can also appreciate the agonies of middle-class children, betrayed and derailed by marital disruption, parked in front of the television set, left alone by overburdened parents struggling to stay afloat in societies that have grown increasingly hostile to families with children.

In the last chapter, we learned how to ameliorate these problems. The methods do exist. Despite the cut-backs of the 1980s, Western Europe is replete with models that work. In countries as diverse as France, the Netherlands and Sweden, Governments know how to intervene on behalf of families, reversing the tide of cumulative causation so that it spirals up instead of down, supporting rather than weakening fragile families, transforming the destinies of vulnerable children. A wealth of evidence supports the claim that State efforts to provide resources and time for parenting can markedly improve the life prospects of children growing up at risk.

If we know what is wrong and how to fix it, the great unanswered question becomes one of resolve: Can governments in some of the world's richest countries muster the political will to move on this front?

The barriers are formidable. To begin with, we need to turn around political cultures whose commitment to free markets leads them to oppose so profoundly the regulation of employer intervention in family life and the spending of public money on children's problems.

If we know what is wrong and how to fix it, the great unanswered question becomes one of resolve: Can governments in some of the world's richest countries muster the political will to move on this front?

Limits and allure of the market

In his *Essays in Persuasion*, John Maynard Keynes described capitalism as that "extraordinary belief that the nastiest of men for the nastiest of motives will somehow work for the benefit of all." In his view, while the "invisible hand" of classical economic theory is capable of maximizing output in the short run, questions of what is just, what is kind or what is wise in the long run cannot be addressed by the market.

The main reason why free-enterprise economies have worked relatively well over the decades is that women have provided vast quantities of free domestic labour. Up until the 1960s, wives and mothers devoted the bulk of their energies to raising children and nurturing families, and in so doing, supplied the human resources for capitalist production.

This system has ceased to function. Women are no longer able to take all the responsibility for family life. Women now comprise 45 per cent of the American workforce and 42 per cent of the British workforce. And their economic contribution — to national economies and to family budgets — is only going to increase as the end of the century draws near. With plummeting male wages and sky-high divorce rates, it is hard to imagine a scenario where large numbers of mothers have the option of staying home with children on a full-time basis.

The solution is to spread the burden around. Husbands and fathers, employers and government, all have to pull their weight. Such a sharing of sacrifice is particularly fair given the fact that in the modern world the rewards of well-developed children are reaped by society at large, not by individual mothers — or fathers.

Historically, this was not nearly so true. In the 18th century, children as young as seven or eight years old contributed significant amounts of labour to the household, and parents were eager to raise a large number of children so that at least some of them survived to support them in their old age.

Neither of these economic incentives for bearing children exists today. Children do not become productive until their late teens or twenties, and even then, rarely contribute to the parental household. Social security and private pensions have replaced children as the major source of material support in old age.

In the modern world, not only are children 'worthless' to their parents, they involve major expenditures. Estimates of the cost of raising a child range from US$200,000 to US$265,000[95] in the United States and from £50,000 to £80,000 in the United Kingdom. In return for such expenditures, "a child is expected to provide love, smiles and emotional satisfaction, but no money or labour."[96] In the late 20th century, "a child is simply not expected to be useful" to his or her parents.[97]

That brings us to a critical Anglo-American dilemma. We expect parents to expend extraordinary amounts of energy and money on raising their children, when it is society at large that reaps the material rewards. The costs are private, the benefits are increasingly public. If you are a 'good' parent and put together the resources and energy to ensure that your child succeeds in school and goes on to complete an expensive college education, you will undoubtedly contribute to 'human capital formation', enhance GNP and help your country compete in the world markets; but in so doing, you will deplete, rather than enhance, your own economic reserves.

As we discovered in the second part of this publication, tighter divorce laws, generous parenting leave and child-care subsidies might well be part of the solution; but whatever the optimum benefits package (and it will vary in different national settings), public policy will have to be used to free up many more resources and much more time for parents — men and women. The critical business of building strong families can no longer be considered a private endeavour, least of all a private female endeavour.

Such ideas resonate in continental Europe. For decades, Swedish social democrats and German social marketeers have worked to refine models of capitalist growth that nurture young people. They are committed to an activist State intervening both to protect and subsidize families with children. Their vision is inspired by notions of social justice, but it also recognizes that over the long haul, high-performing economies are dependent upon strong families. Children are 100 per cent of the future; if they are neglected, stagnation and decline are inevitable.

The reason that these arguments need to be made again in the 1990s is that unfettered markets have acquired new allure. Hard on the heels of British and American conservative successes in discrediting government during the 1980s, the collapse of communist regimes in Central and Eastern Europe and the Soviet Union from 1989 to 1991 seemed to confirm the "victory of economic and political liberalism."[98]

Large segments of public opinion came to believe that free enterprise is intrinsically good, while State action is intrinsically bad. In this new climate of opinion, the Anglo-American model of free-wheeling capitalism is particularly admired. In the words of London's *Financial Times*: "For millions around the world, the American flag is a symbol of an economic and social system that works. No country is more committed to personal freedom and the market economy than the United States, and no country offers the enterprising individual greater opportunity."[99]

Of course, free markets, American style, have not 'worked' for children. They have been a disaster, but that does not seem to have diminished the appeal of the American model. In large numbers of countries, including Western European ones, the economic landscape is newly littered with privatization schemes, shrinking public budgets and apologetic bureaucrats. In countries as committed to the well-being of children as the Netherlands and Sweden, well-established, effective programmes of family support are being dismantled in the name of freeing markets and returning responsibility to parents. Even in Sweden, a 15-billion-kronor package of health and public service cuts, many of which will harm children, is on the agenda.

The small country of New Zealand offers a cautionary tale.[100] Its recent history provides sobering evidence of the American model's ability to wreak havoc in both the economic and social spheres. Long regarded as one of the world's most enlightened social democracies, New Zealand has, since 1984, demolished a cradle-to-grave social welfare system in the name of economic efficiency. Nevertheless, untrammelled markets have not produced vigorous growth. On the contrary, eight years of stringent monetarist policies have produced massive unemployment, rising crime rates, a widening gap between rich and poor, and a declining GDP. Between 1985 and 1990, New Zealand's GNP fell by 0.7 per cent, the worst record of any industrialized country, while unemployment more than doubled. The deterioration in living standards has been particularly severe among families with children, with predictable results. New Zealand now has the highest youth suicide rate among industrialized countries, and reported cases of child abuse have doubled since 1985.

Throughout the Anglo-American world the pattern is the same. Unfettered markets do not seem to work on either the social or the economic front. After approximately a decade of market forces, growth rates in the increasingly 'private' economies of Australia, Canada, New Zealand, the United Kingdom and the United States stubbornly lag behind

We expect parents to expend extraordinary amounts of energy and money on raising their children, when it is society at large that reaps the material rewards.

the supposedly welfare-ridden, inefficient economies of Europe.

How can we expose this love affair with free markets and take (or retake) collective responsibility for our children? The answer is simple. We must remind ourselves of the appalling costs of child neglect. Any nation that allows large numbers of its children to grow up in poverty, afflicted by poor health, handicapped by inferior education, deserted by fathers and cut adrift by society, is asking for economic stagnation and social chaos, and will get it — richly deserved.

Harnessing enlightened self-interest

In the United Kingdom and the United States, business leaders are beginning to realize that the swelling tide of child neglect has potentially disastrous consequences not only for the individual child but for society as a whole. Deprived, undereducated children grow into problem-ridden youngsters who are extremely difficult to absorb into the modern workforce.

Young drug users in New Zealand reflect the high cost of monetary policies that have resulted in rising levels of unemployment, crime and child abuse.

Human capital requirements are escalating. The skill needs of advanced industrial economies are moving rapidly up the scale, "with most new jobs demanding more education and higher levels of language, math and reasoning skills."[101] Qualifications for jobs, even low-wage jobs, are rising. Estimates are that by the late 1990s the average job will require a full year more education than was true in the late 1980s.

The United States — or New Zealand, for that matter — should clearly invest more in education. Schools can and should do more to prepare youngsters for productive employment, but they will continue to fall short of the mark unless those societies also support parents and give them the time and resources to do better by their children.

The education system cannot compensate for the tasks overburdened parents no longer perform. Chicago sociologist James Coleman has shown that across a wide range of subjects in literature and science, "the total effect of home background is considerably greater than the total effect of school variables." Overall, the home is almost twice as powerful as the school in determining student achievement at age 14.[102]

Given chaos on the home front, youngsters in Anglo-American cultures — particularly in the United Kingdom and the United States — find it difficult to do well in school. A 1989 study by the International

Assessment of Math and Science, which examined students in 11 advanced industrial countries, showed American students coming in last and British students next to last. Indeed, less than half of American 17-year-olds can correctly determine whether 87 per cent of 10 is greater than, less than, or equal to 10; nor can they determine the area of a rectangle. Some 35 per cent of American eleventh-graders write at or below the following level: "I have been experience at cleaning house Ive also work at a pool for I love keeping things neat organized and clean. Im very social Ill get to know people really fast."[103]

Such an impressive level of educational failure has serious repercussions in the labour market. In 1987, New York Telephone had to test 57,000 people before it could find 2,100 who were well educated enough for entry-level jobs as operators or repair technicians. IBM discovered after installing millions of dollars worth of sophisticated equipment in its Burlington, Vermont factories that it had to teach high-school algebra to workers before they could handle the new technology. Xerox's Chairman, David Kearns, estimated that United States industry spends US$25 billion a year on remedial education for workers.

The stakes are enormous. It is not just a question of whether Xerox will grow at 2 per cent or 4 per cent a year, it is a question of whether a shortfall in skills and in labour productivity will trigger a permanent decline in the American productive potential. The fact is, human capital is now the most important factor of production.

Children are 100 per cent of the future; if they are neglected, stagnation and decline are inevitable.

As economies become international, a nation's most important competitive asset becomes the skills and cumulative learning of its workforce. The very process of globalization makes this true, since every factor of production other than workforce skills can now be duplicated anywhere in the world. In the words of political economist Robert Reich, "Capital now sloshes freely across international boundaries, so much so that the cost of capital in different countries is rapidly converging. State-of-the-art factories can be erected anywhere. The latest technologies flow from computers in one nation, up to satellites parked in space, then back down to computers in another nation — all at the speed of electronic impulses. It is all fungible: capital, technology, raw materials, information — all, except for one thing, the most critical part, the one element that is unique about a nation: its workforce."[104]

In fact, because all of the other factors of production can move so easily around the world, a workforce that is knowledgeable and skilled at doing complex things sets up a 'virtuous circle'. High-calibre workers attract global corporations, which invest and give the workers well-paid jobs; high-productivity workers, in turn, further develop through on-the-job training and experience. As skills become more sophisticated and experience accumulates, "a nation's citizens add greater and greater value to the world — and command greater and greater compensation from the world — improving the country's standard of living."

If a 'virtuous circle' is operating in France and Sweden — nations that have invested time and money in their children — a 'vicious circle' operates in the United Kingdom and the United States, where child neglect has undermined human capital formation and frightened away potential

investment. A 1991 survey by the *Harvard Business Review* shows corporate executives in countries as diverse as Argentina, Germany and Italy giving enormous weight to human resources in decisions about where to site new investment.[105]

The best news of the early 1990s is that the private sector has seen the writing on the wall and is beginning to mobilize political energy. For example, in the United States, the Committee for Economic Development, a think-tank comprising 200 business leaders, has begun to lobby hard for massively increased public investment in programmes such as Headstart.

In the United Kingdom, Opportunity 2000, a consortium of 15 large corporations, is newly promoting child-care subsidies for working parents. To use the eloquent words of the Committee for Economic Development: "The nation cannot continue to compete and prosper in the global arena when more than a fifth of our children live in poverty and a third grow up in ignorance ... If we continue to squander the talents of millions of our children, America will become a nation of limited human potential. It would be tragic if we allowed this to happen."[106] Not only is it tragic for the United States, but also tragic for the profitability of individual corporations — for increasingly, the competitive strength of any business enterprise depends on the calibre of its human capital.

The private sector is rarely in the vanguard of social policy, but when it comes to human resources, the statistics and the trend indicators speak with an urgency that is hard to ignore. Corporate executives understand that the welfare of children cannot be left to the vagaries of the private market, because on the backs of these children rides the future prosperity of nations — and firms.

It seems that in the waning years of the 20th century, doing what is right for our children and what is necessary to save our collective skins will finally come together: Conscience and convenience will converge.

Are governments in the rich world able to learn from this hard-headed investment logic? Will a human capital frame of reference enable countries such as the United Kingdom and the United States to move on this front?

Arguing the case for enlightened self-interest is clearly a critical first step. It is important to show taxpayers that neglecting children is an extremely expensive proposition. In the United States, for example, very few citizens understand that they are already picking up the tab for damaged children — just one class of high school drop-outs costs the country US$242 million in forgone earnings. Compassion, it turns out, is a whole lot cheaper than callousness.

But conjuring up political will is a much more complicated exercise than cost-benefit analysis. In the Anglo-American world, investing in children involves nothing less than turning around political cultures that have become deeply antagonistic to government action. In the wake of the Reagan-Thatcher revolutions, politicians are loath to intervene no matter how worthy the cause or effective the programme. Concerted action to save our children is therefore contingent upon a new type of leadership. If US President Bill Clinton — or any other leader — can convince the electorate that a 'reinvented' government is capable of promoting investment and taking responsibility for the future, then, and only then, can we create the conditions that will allow our children to thrive.

It seems that in the waning years of the 20th century, doing what is right for our children and what is necessary to save our collective skins will finally come together: Conscience and convenience will converge.

NOTES

[1] Smeeding, Timothy M., 'The War on Poverty: What Worked?', 25 September 1991, testimony prepared for the Joint Economic Committee, US Congress. See also: John Coder, Lee Rainwater and Timothy Smeeding, *American Economic Association Papers and Proceedings,* 'Inequality Among Children and Elderly in Ten Modern Nations: The United States in an International Context', American Economic Association, Nashville, Tenn., May 1989, p. 323.

[2] Innocenti Occasional Papers, UNICEF, International Child Development Centre, Florence, 1990. Cornia, Giovanni Andrea, 'Child Poverty and Deprivation in Industrialized Countries: Recent Trends and Policy Options' (No. 2, p. 29). Jonathan Bradshaw, 'Child Poverty and Deprivation in the UK' (No. 8, p. 8). Using a different measure, Bradshaw shows a startling rise in child poverty in the UK; in his study the child poverty rate rises from 9 per cent in 1980 to 18 per cent in 1985.

[3] National Commission on the Role of the School and the Community in Improving Adolescent Health, *Code Blue: Uniting for Healthier Youth*, National Association of State Boards of Education and the American Medical Association, Washington, D.C., 1990, p. 3.

[4] United Nations Children's Fund (UNICEF), *The State of the World's Children 1993*, Oxford University Press, 1992, p. 58.

[5] Smeeding, Timothy M., 'The Debt, the Deficit and Disadvantaged Children: Generational Impacts and Age, Period and Cohort Effects', in *The Debt and the Twin Deficits Debate*, ed. James M. Rock, Bristlecone Books/Mayfield, Mountain View, California, 1991, p. 47.

[6] Ng, Edward, 'Children and Elderly People: Sharing Public Income Resources', *Canadian Social Trends*, Statistics Canada, Summer 1992, p. 15.

[7] Fuchs, Victor R., *Women's Quest for Economic Equality,* Harvard University Press, Cambridge, Mass., 1988, p. 111.

[8] Schor, Juliet B., *The Overworked American: The Unexpected Decline of Leisure*, Basic Books, New York, 1992, p. 28.

[9] Hewitt, Patricia, *About Time: The Revolution in Work and Family Life*, IPPR Rivers Oram Press, London, 1993, p. 16. These figures refer to average male manual workers' hours.

[10] Cornia, op. cit., pp. 1-27 for a discussion of these trend lines.

[11] National Commission on the Role of the School and the Community in Improving Adolescent Health, op. cit. p. 3.

[12] Telephone interviews, Bob Cleveland, US Bureau of the Census, 30 April and 22 September 1990.

[13] Quoted in Susan Champlin Taylor, 'A Promise at Risk', *Modern Maturity*, August-September 1989, p. 36.

[14] Organisation for Economic Co-operation and Development, *Historical Statistics, 1960-1989*, Paris, 1991.

[15] Fuchs, op. cit., pp. 104-106.

[16] Mattox, William R. Jr., 'The Family Time Famine', *Family Policy*, 3, No. 1, The Family Research Council, 1990, p. 2.

[17] Chakravarty, Subrata N., and Weisman, Katherine, 'Consuming Our Children?', *Forbes*, 14 November 1988, p. 228.

[18] Newton, John, *All in One Place: The British Housing Story, 1971-90*, Catholic Housing Aid Society, London, 1991, pp. 35-39.

[19] Gibbs, Nancy, 'How America Has Run Out of Time', *Time*, 24 April, 1989, p. 59.

[20] Bennett, Amanda, 'Early to Bed ... A Look at the CEO Workweek', *The Wall Street Journal*, 20 March 1987, p. 22D; Pamela Mendels, 'Eyes Are Off the Clock', *Newsday*, 19 August 1990, p. 58.

[21] Moss Kanter, Rosabeth, *When Giants Learn to Dance: Mastering the Challenges of Strategy, Management and Careers in the 1990s*, Simon & Schuster, New York, 1989, p. 271.

[22] Ibid., p. 270.

[23] *The Independent*, 25 February 1992.

[24] Brooks, Andrée Aelion, *Children of Fast-Track Parents*, Viking, New York, 1989, pp. 29-30.

25 Richardson, J. L., et al., 'Substance Use Among Eighth-Grade Students Who Take Care of Themselves After School', *Pediatrics*, 84, No. 3, September 1989, pp. 556-566.

26 *Studies in Marriage and the Family*, US Bureau of the Census, Current Population Reports, Series P-23, No. 162, June 1989, p. 5.

27 *Child Support and Alimony: 1987*, US Bureau of the Census, Current Population Reports, Series P-23, No. 167, June 1990, pp. 3-7.

28 Duncan, Greg J., and Hoffmann, Saul D., 'A Reconsideration of the Economic Consequences of Marital Dissolution', *Demography*, 22, No. 4, November 1986, pp. 485-497.

29 Furstenberg, Frank F. Jr., and Mullan Harris, Kathleen, 'The Disappearing Father? Divorce and the Waning Significance of Biological Parenthood', draft, Department of Sociology, University of Pennsylvania, March 1990.

30 Quoted in Tamar Lewin, 'Father's Vanishing Act Called Common Drama', *The New York Times*, 4 June 1990, p. A18.

31 Velez, Carmen Noemi, and Cohen, Patricia, 'Suicidal Behavior in a Community Sample of Children: Maternal and Youth Reports', *Journal of the American Academy of Child and Adolescent Psychiatry*, 27, No. 3, May 1988, pp. 349-356.

32 Cited in Nicholas Davidson, 'Life Without Father', *Policy Review*, No. 51, Winter 1990, p. 41.

33 Fitzgerald Krein, Sheila, and Beller, Andrea H., 'Educational Attainment of Children from Single-Parent Families: Differences by Exposure, Gender and Race', *Demography*, 25, No. 2, May 1988, pp. 221-233.

34 Kagan, Jerome, *The Nature of the Child*, Basic Books, New York, 1984, p. 108.

35 Smeeding, Timothy M., 'The War on Poverty: What Worked?', 25 September 1991, testimony prepared for the Joint Economic Committee, US Congress.

36 For an analysis of US government policy towards the young and the old, see discussion in Sylvia Ann Hewlett, *When the Bough Breaks: The Cost of Neglecting our Children*, HarperCollins, New York, 1992, Chapter 5.

37 Ng, Edward, op. cit., p. 14.

38 Smeeding, Timothy M., op. cit.

39 Leonard, Paul A., Colbeare, Cushing N., and Lazere, Edward B., 'A Place to Call Home: The Crisis in Housing for the Poor', Center on Budget and Policy Priorities, Washington, D.C., April 1989, pp. xiv, 28-31.

40 Steinbach, Carol F., and Peirce, Neal R., 'Picking Up Hammers', *National Journal*, 6 June 1987, p. 1465.

41 Meyer, Jack A., and Moon, Marilyn, 'Health Care Spending on Children and the Elderly', in *The Vulnerable*, eds. Palmer, Smeeding, Torrey, Urban Institute Press, Washington, D.C., 1988, p. 179.

42 National Commission to Prevent Infant Mortality, 'Infant Mortality Fact Sheet,' January 1990.

43 Ibid.

44 Cornia, Giovanni Andrea, op. cit, p. 15.

45 See discussion in Sylvia Ann Hewlett, *A Lesser Life: The Myth of Women's Liberation in America*, Morrow, New York, 1986, pp. 70-109.

46 Holmes, Steven A., 'Bush Vetoes Bill on Family Leave', *The New York Times*, 30 June 1990, p. A9.

47 Equal Opportunities Commission, *Women and Men in Britain,* HMSO, London, 1991, p. 25.

48 *Women in Australia*, Report to the United Nations Convention on the Elimination of All Forms of Discrimination Against Women, June 1992, p. 128.

49 Zigler, Edward F., and Frank, Meryl, eds., *The Parental Leave Crisis: Toward a New National Policy*, Yale University Press, New Haven, Conn., 1988, p. xix.

50 Glendon, Mary Ann, *Abortion and Divorce in Western Law: American Failures, European Challenges,* Harvard University Press, Cambridge, Mass., 1987, p. 142.

51 Testimony of Dr. Lenora Cole Alexander, director of the Women's Bureau, US Department of Labor, before the Joint Economic Committee of the US Congress, 3 April 1984, p. 9.

52 Haggstrom, Gus W., et. al., 'Changes in the Life Styles of New Parents', Rand Corporation, Santa Monica, Calif., December 1984, p. 61.

53 Packard, Vance, *Our Endangered Children: Growing Up in a Changing World*, Little, Brown, New York, 1983, p. 56.

54 Hewlett, Sylvia Ann, *A Lesser Life*, p. 374.

55 The Dutch Cross Society is an association promoting maternal and child health care as well as home nursing for the sick, disabled and elderly. It is organized on a national, regional and local basis, and two thirds of all Dutch families are members.

56 Williams, Bret C., and Miller, C. Arden, *Preventive Health Care for Young Children: Findings from a 10-Country Study and Directions for United States Policy*, National Center for Clinical Infant Programs, Washington, D.C., 1991, p. 26.

57 Miller, C. Arden, *Maternal Health and Infant Survival*, National Center for Clinical Infant Programs, Washington, D.C., 1987, p. 24.

58 'Maternity Home Care and Related Services on Offer by the Dutch Cross Society', National Association for Community Nursing and Home Help Services, Bunnick, Netherlands, 1991, pp. 12-13.

59 Ibid., p. 12.

60 The Swedish Institute, 'Fact Sheets on Sweden: Child Care in Sweden', March 1990.

61 National Social Insurance Board, Statistical Division, *Social Insurance Statistics: Facts 1991*, National Social Insurance Board, December 1991, Stockholm, pp. 25-29.

62 'By Your Leave, Europe', *The Economist*, 22 August 1987, p. 46, and *Women in Australia*, 1992, p. 129.

63 The Swedish Institute, 'Fact Sheets on Sweden: Social Insurance in Sweden', January 1991.

64 Cutler, Blayne, 'The Swedish Example', *American Demographics*, Vol. 11, No. 4, April 1989, p. 70.

65 *The Progress of Nations*, UNICEF, New York, 1993, p. 51.

66 Kamerman, Sheila B., 'Child Care Policies and Programs: An International Overview', *Journal of Social Issues*, Vol. 47, No. 2, 1991, p. 193.

67 Leprince, Frederique, in *Day Care for Young Children: International Perspec-tives*, Edward C. Melhuish and Peter Moss, eds., Routledge, London, 1991, p. 12.

68 *Childcare in the European Communities, 1985-90*, Commission of the European Community, No. 31, Brussels, August 1990, p. 19.

69 *L'Enfant dans la vie*, 1986.

70 Baudelot, Olga, 'Child Care in France', in Sylvia Ann Hewlett, Alice S. Ilchman, and John J. Sweeney, *Family and Work: Bridging the Gap*, Ballinger, Cambridge, Mass., 1986, p. 49.

71 Holtermann, Sally, *Investing in Young Children: Costing an Education and Day Care Service*, National Children's Bureau, London, 1992.

72 Cohen, Bronwen, and Fraser, Neil, *Childcare in a Modern Welfare State: Towards a New National Policy*, Institute of Public Policy Research, London, 1991.

73 Hansard, H.L., Vol. 502, Col. 488.

74 *Children in Care*, House of Commons Social Services Select Committee Report, London, 1984.

75 Parton, Nigel, *Governing the Family: Child Care, Child Protection and the State*, Macmillan, 1991, p. 75.

76 *The Guardian*, 26 February 1992, p. 23.

77 Frost, Nick, and Stein, Mike, 'The Politics of the Children Act', *Childright*, No. 68, July/August 1990, pp. 17-19.

78 Glendon, Mary Ann, op. cit., p. 105.

79 Ibid., p. 84.

80 Ibid., p. 85.

81 Ibid., p. 86. The generosity of the Swedish benefit-service package is described in S. Kamerman and A. Kahn, *Income transfers for Families with Children: An Eight-Country Study*, Temple University Press, Philadelphia, 1983.

82 Quoted in Lenore J. Weitzman, *The Marriage Contract*, The Free Press, New York, 1981, p. 152.

83 See discussion in Hewlett, *When the Bough Breaks*, pp. 322-323.

84 *Bulletin*, London, Family Policy Studies Centre, December 1991, p. 8.

85 *OECD Observer*, 'Labour Markets in the 1990s: OECD Employment Outlook', Paris, October/November 1990.

86 Dingwall, James, 'A Labor Crisis Looms', D & B Reports, May/June 1989, p. 63.

87 *Business Week*, 19 September 1988.

88 Burud, Sandra L., Aschbacker, Pamela R., and McCroskey, Jacquelyn, *Employer Supported Child Care: Investing in Human Resources*, Auburn House, Dover, Mass., 1984, pp. 22-26.

89 Ransom, Cynthia, Aschbacker, Pamela R., and Burud, Sandra L., 'The Return in the Child-Care Investment', *Personnel Administrator*, October 1989, pp. 54-58. Nationwide, mothers of preschool children have a very high absentee rate—11.5 per cent, compared with 5.8 per cent for married women with no children. See Joseph R. Meisenheimer II, 'Employee Absences in 1989: A New Look at Data from the CBS', *Monthly Labor Review*, 113, No. 8, August 1990, p. 29.

90 Warne, Lynne M., 'News Release', Honeywell Inc., Minneapolis, Minn., 3 August 1989.

91 Phillips, J. Douglas, 'Employee Turnover and the Bottom Line', working paper, Merck & Co. Inc., February 1989, p. 2.

92 Ibid., p. 6.

93 Smith, Michael, 'Nursery Lesson for Employers on Childcare', The *Financial Times*, 24 February 1989, p. 7.

94 Telephone interview, Ted Childs, Director, Work-Life Program, IBM, 8 March 1991.

95 According to Sheila Kamerman, "The prototypical American family with two children, a working father and a part-time working mother ... can expect to spend about $200,000 per child up to age 18." See book review by Sheila B. Kamerman of Thomas J. Espenshade's *Investing in Children: New Estimates of Parental Expenditures*, The Urban Institute Press, Washington, D.C., 1984, in *Social Work*, May-June 1986, Vol. 31, No. 3, p. 227. More recently *Money* magazine, using Department of Agriculture figures, estimated that the average family earning $50,000 or more a year will spend $265,249 to feed, clothe and shelter a child up to age 22. See Andrea Rock, 'Can You Afford Your Kids?', *Money*, July 1990, Vol. 19, No. 7, pp. 88-99.

96 Zelizer, Viviana A., *Pricing the Priceless Child: The Changing Social Value of Children*, Basic Books Inc., New York, 1985, p. 3.

97 Ibid., p. 4.

98 Fukuyama, Francis, 'The End of History', *The National Interest*, No. 16, Summer 1989, p 3.

99 *The Financial Times*, 20 April 1990, p. 26.

100 'A Third World New Zealand?', *Time*, 16 December 1991, pp. 20-25.

101 Johnston, William B., and Packer, Arnold H., *Workforce 2000: Work and Workers for the 21st Century*, Hudson Institute, Indianapolis, 1987, p. 102.

102 Coleman, James S., US Department of Health, Education and Welfare, National Institute of Education, 'Effects of School on Learning: The IEA Findings', presented at a Conference on Educational Achievement, Harvard University, November 1973, p. 40.

103 Ehrlich, Elizabeth, 'America's Schools Still Aren't Making the Grade', *Business Week*, 19 September 1988, p. 132.

104 Reich, Robert B., 'Who is Us?', *Harvard Business Review*, 68, No. 1, January-February 1990, p. 59.

105 Ohmae, K., et. al., 'The Boundaries of Business: Commentaries from the Experts', *Harvard Business Review*, Cambridge, Mass., July-August 1991, p. 127.

106 Committee for Economic Development, 'Children in Need, Investment Strategies for the Educationally Disadvantaged', CED, Washington, D.C., 1987, p. 3.

Photo credits

P. vi: Raissa Page/Format

P. 4:   Gale Zucker/Stock Boston

P. 9:   Peter Menzel/Stock Boston

P. 10: Gale Zucker/Stock Boston

P. 14: Mike Mazzaschi/Stock Boston

P. 18: Glen Korengold/Stock Boston

P. 20: Stephen Shames/Matrix

P. 23: Stephen Shames/Matrix

P. 24: Francesco Zizola

P. 25: Stephen Shames/Matrix

P. 28: Brenda Prince/Format

P. 29: Francesco Zizola

P. 30: Stig Nilsson/Pressen Bild

P. 34: Paul Hansen/Pressens Bild

P. 37: Guy Le Querrec/Magnum

P. 38: Jean-Claude Lejeune/Stock Boston

P. 41: Brenda Prince/Stock Boston

P. 44: Owen Franken/Stock Boston

P. 47: Frances Cox/Stock Boston

P. 50: David Hurn/Magnum

P. 54: *The Wellington Evening Post*

P. 56: Stephen Shames/Matrix

Cover illustration: Michelle Siegel